LEAD TO GOLD

An entrepreneur's guide to transition, transformation and evolution

"My heart is afraid that it will have to suffer," the boy told the alchemist one night as they looked up at the moonless sky.

"Tell your heart that the fear of suffering is worse than the suffering itself. And that no heart has ever suffered when it goes in search of its dreams."

Paulo Coelho, The Alchemist

Video Message from the Author

Leadtogoldbook.com/messagefromtheauthor

Disclaimer

The names of some of the people in my corporate stories have been changed out of respect to those people and to protect their identities. I also realize this is my story and perspective and they may clearly have a different version and that I have never fully taken the time to vet and compare notes. Nor would I in these circumstances.

Acknowledgement

Since this is my first effort at writing an acknowledgment section for a book, I wasn't sure exactly where to start and who to thank since there are so many. But I do know how to say thank you. I've said thank you millions of times over my life in general, but always to the many people who have helped me, inspired me, guided me and motivated me to be the best I could possibly be on my path. I am eternally grateful to all of those many people, and if you're reading this book you know who you are if you've touched my life in some way. I appreciate it and please know that some piece of your kind gesture, your wisdom, your generosity, your expertise, your inspiration and our kindred spirits are in some way and somehow reflected throughout this book!

I do want to specifically thank my wife Mary Lou, who had my heart and soul from the first moment I met her and still does. I love you and I'm so grateful we are on this path and journey together over all these many years. The bumps, hurdles and sometimes tragedies were always overshadowed by our glorious love for each other and our common faith in a higher power - always guiding us, always providing.

To my parents Al and Jackie Rodgers who have been married 55 years, raised five boys into men and who continually set the example as the utmost respected role models. You both have always been the original teachers for me of understanding and learning how to turn lead into gold. Thank you for my life and for who you are. I love you both with deep respect and appreciation.

And while I'm on the family subject, I can't help but do a shout out to my two children Nicole and PJ, as well as grandkids Sarah & Ema and soon-to-be grandbaby boy Cove Augestine. My four brothers Jay, Mike, Barry and Kenny and all of my immediate family from coast-to-coast, I love you all. You have all given me a unique imprint on my being, outlook, attitudes and perspectives. You have been great teachers for me in all of life's lessons that are to be explored on this planet. It may not always be said in the right words, time or way but please know I realize you will be some of the greatest gold I ever come across. I am grateful in that!

I've been so blessed to have so many wonderful mentors along the way. Many of them are the reasons I've sought this path of writing, expressing some of my views and insights. Their own great writings, leadership, mentoring and paving the way while inspiring others have fueled part of my desire. Some very specific mentors have helped me by recommending this book, offering content, videos and bonuses for the reader along with so much more; for this I'm humbled and so grateful. I appreciate and value you all!

I need to point out a long-term friend and mentor Brian Tracy whose amazing career, books, seminars and videos have inspired millions. I've been so blessed to have Brian as a friend and mentor for over 12 years now. Not only did Brian help me with advice and guidance, promotion and a bonus book, but he graciously wrote the foreword in this book. He is a true role model and a wise and kind man!

To Marshall Goldsmith, the world-renowned top executive coach in the world and serial New York Times best-selling author. He has been a constant friend, mentor and someone who gives sage advice that I will always respect and cherish. Thank you for your expertise, wisdom, shining example and generous heart.

Other mentors and friends who always go the extra mile for me were leaders like Mark Thompson who is an author, speaker and serial entrepreneur who not only amazes and inspires me, but many throughout the world doing such good for so many.

Greg and Allyn Reid, founders of the amazing Secret Knock workshops, authors and Secret of Happiness founders. They give with grace and ease.

John Assaraf successful serial entrepreneur, mind and brain expert as well as one of the original contributors to the hit book "The Secret" has always been a friend whose advice and guidance I have cherished and will continue to do so. He has truly mastered manifesting and shows others how to create the lives they desire.

Dr. Gary Ranker, global coach, successful author and specialist in politics in the workplace has for years been so gracious to me with his time, great advice, open heart and global perspectives. As I have transitioned and transformed through the years, Gary has been a sound voice of reason.

Steve Games who is reflected in my book and story has been a mentor and friend for over 20 years. His ability to dream, inspire, lead, create, shake up, energize and manifest in his life and indirectly the lives of others, is a truly magical gift. Steve and his partner Nyda Jones Church, and their team, not only helped create one of the most successful real estate companies in the United States, but his entrepreneurial drive and spirit helped reshape a small piece of another country's coastline, spirit and economy. I am forever grateful to him for allowing me a path and showing me how to dream bigger and live life with even more gusto!

There are so many others whose kindness, generosity and support have been invaluable to me as I maneuvered this thing called life. I am touched in awe of all the many ways people with giving and sincere hearts can dramatically affect the lives of others. There are too many to list here, but I have added an additional page in the back of this book titled "Ambassadors." I want to acknowledge those who made the extra effort to be of value in my life and now in the lives of even more readers of this book.

A book does not get written on its own. There are so many people that help contribute to the author from editors, graphic artist, marketing people and specialized advisors. Marilyn McLeod not only helped me edit this book but in some sections helped me co-write pieces when I was stuck. Thank you Marilyn for your collaboration, your skills, talents and your curious and miraculous nature. You have had your own historic path along the way mastering turning lead in the gold. I'm so glad my first book had part of your essence and unique imprint. Sarah Pugh, my transplanted niece from the east coast to the west who helped edit with another set of eyes and valued unique perspective that I was so grateful to have on our path. Your own unique writing talent was something that came at the right time.

In addition, Lane Ethridge and Haris Reis of "Changing Lanes" helped us towards the end of the process fine-tune the book and format it to create our end product. Thank you guys for your amazing can-do attitude and prompt, positive approach to what seemed a daunting task. You helped fuel it toward the finish and that is the coolest thing of all!

At the end of the day I realize it's impossible to thank everyone I should be thanking. But as I stated above I hope everyone knows as you read this book or listen to the upcoming audio that you will know in your heart and mind that the collective value of many reside in this book. I have been shaped and inspired by all I have met and been guided by many that have helped me on my journey. The many gifts, wisdom and the divine interventions that I know have come in the form of my family and meeting my cherished friends along the way are what make me who I am.

The final expression of my gratitude is to my higher power, God, that is the sum all that is in all things in all universes. I am in deep desire to serve You to the highest by serving others. I will follow my path and await your further promptings. The essence of this relationship is at the core of my personal legend and I am in awe of the beauty this offers and reflects daily in my life and the lives of others.

Much Gratitude,
Stephen D. Rodgers

"In his very practical book *Lead to gold*, Steve shares his journey through both the corporate and entrepreneurial arenas, and his success through many ups and downs." Using his gifts as an inspirational leader, he engages the reader with insights into setting one's path, and then building on that foundation through step by step advice about how to implement the necessary tasks of starting and building a successful small business."

- Marshall Goldsmith
  Voted Top 5 Executive Business Coach Global Gurus
  Thinkers 50 list
  NY Times Best Selling Author Triggers, MOJO, "What Got You Here, Won't Get You There"

Lead to gold is an exceptional book filled with real life lessons that any entrepreneur who is serious about success can devour and learn from. Steve shares his highs, lows, ups and downs in a way that will empower to relentlessly go after your biggest goals and dreams!

- John Assaraf, Chairman & CEO, NeuroGym, added to the book the Secret, Wrote the book "The Answer", Having it all and various bestselling books.

Lead to gold is Priceless. It reveals the trade secrets of how to transition and transform your life to your advantage. Steve Rodgers walks his talk. I have witnessed him transform his health, mind body and soul to the highest levels of performance. Steve Rodgers and his work is inspirational for all looking to expand their business and personal quality of life. Don't miss out, get on board with *Lead to gold*.

- Barnet G. Meltzer, M.D., F.A.A.F.P.
  pioneer and expert physician in holistic and
  preventative medicine. Author, talk show host,
  speaker, Diplomate American Board of Family
  Practice

"I was so excited to see Steve get his first book published! I am sure it is the first of many to be written. His insights and story from rising up through the ranks of the corporate world to become the CEO of a Warren Buffett Berkshire Hathaway company is impressive. And his transition then into his true path as an entrepreneur is quite a feat that he did with grace and gusto. His writings and speaking will surely help many get better at what they do, or help them find their true path if they are still searching. I highly recommend this book to anyone who appreciates following in the footsteps of a successful businessman who combines heart with practical strategies in a step by step format."

Mark Thompson
NY Times bestselling Author, Serial Midas touch
investor
Former Chief of Staff Charles Schwab
Worked side by side Steve Jobs, Charles Schwab, and
Richard Branson

"You won't want to miss this *Lead to gold* opportunity. Do yourself a favor and save yourself valuable time and money by reading this practical advice from Steve Rodgers' personal and business experience. Steve takes you step by step through the wisdom he's distilled from hard and valuable experience. It doesn't get any better than this in having someone help you avoid many of the hurdles and go right for the gold!"

- Bill Walsh CEO & Founder Power Team USA
  Voted top 10 business coaches in the US by Global Gurus
  Powerteam International

'Steve is the world's authority on turning adversity into opportunities - and is one of life's great champions.'

- Greg S Reid, author Think and Grow Rich series. Secret Knock Workshops, Serial entrepreneur, speaker

"I have just read an advance copy of Steve Rodger's newest book and am amazed at how relevant and useful his writing is for many of us. It is targeted towards those who are or wish to be entrepreneurs, but the philosophy is so positive and strong I think most of us can gain from reading his book.I am struck by how thoroughly authentic and honest Steve is in describing his journey, actually chronicling how he has remained such a positive successful values driven person through all the ups and downs of life. What he shares can be an excellent model to strive for - as most of us also encounter problems, not just success in our lives.Steve is truly inspirational and if there is one value in reading the book is that fact - his writings are so honest, his struggles so easy to identify with for many of us, and his ability to rise above it all and demonstrate his resilience is amazing. I doubt that anyone who reads Steve's book will go away unchanged. They will feel inspired to reach for more, to become more of the best they can be.

- Dr. Gary Ranker
  Global CEO Coach, speaker

"An inspiring book from a very upbeat, thoughtful writer. Loaded with solid & proven advice, this empowering book is true alchemy, enabling readers to manifest their dreams into reality! Beautifully written & with a wonderful spiritual component as an elixir."

- Dr. Scott & Shannon Peck, Authors, "The Love You Deserve" & "Liberating Your Magnificence"

You can learn from a guru or you can learn from someone who has lived it, survived it and is teaching about it. Give yourself a shot at success and read *Lead to gold*.

- Mrs. Allyn Reid, Publisher, Producer and Mrs. San Diego 2015. Cofounder of Secret Knock workshops

"I have been privileged to share the stage, learn from, mentor, be mentored, and partner with leading global business authorities. Our company helps thousands of business owners all over the world and I always look for cutting edge material for our Customers and our team. I have met Steve Rodgers while he was leading a major real estate brand and during his transition into the consulting and coaching industries. Steve comes from the real world with years of experience as a high profile CEO plus the wisdom he acquired by working with many business leaders which endorse him without question on this book because of his caliber. He walks the talk and made changes in his own career and will help you more effectively navigate the decisions and transitions you will inevitably have to make in a fast changing business world. My core value is Freedom. I think having the ability to make the right timely choices and transitions can be the difference between living a life of compromise and a life of Freedom and inspiration and Steve's book will help you to ask yourself important questions in that regard and open your mind to the possible."

- Fabrice BEILLARD
  Globally acclaimed Business Optimization Expert, Best Selling Author, International Speaker

What a great and very powerful book. Steve Rogers is a business genius.

You truly can have all the success you desire in life. I love this book and the simple examples to continue to evolve in your own life. This book struck an awaking in me and I highly recommend you reading it now and share it with your business associates and friends.

- Steven E. Schmitt, Founder of Law of positivity
  Author, Entrepreneur, media expert

"This fast-moving, enjoyable book takes you on a journey to greater success, loaded with ideas, strategies and inspiration that can transform your life."

- Brian S. Tracy
  World renowned speaker and over 70 bestselling books written consulted for more than 1,000 companies and addressed more than 5,000,000 people in 5,000 talks and seminars throughout the world

Grandma said "people are like teabags- you don't know how strong they are till you dip them in hot water." Steve Rodgers has been there and proves he is strong and in this compellingly instructive book reveals exactly how to leverage difficult transition (lead) into transformation (gold). One powerful book.

- David M. Corbin coach, keynote speaker, author ILLUMINATE, Preventing Brand Slaughter, ReSanity

"I've known Steve for over 20 years. Like me, Steve has gone through his own personal setbacks and rebuilt even stronger each time. In *Lead to gold* you'll follow his trials and triumphs, and even better, his secrets to turning adversity to gold. If you want to make the big leap to a better life and career, I encourage you to read this book. It will guide you through both the highs and lows of being in business. It will also show you how to stay positive and encouraged in life even in the most difficult of circumstances. Steve is truly one of the most resilient and positive people I have ever met in my life and this book reflects that and more!"

- Marie Jo Atkins San Diego top Real Estate agent Over 1 billion dollars in real estate sold. Pacific Sotheby's Poway California

"After ten years of being mentored and coached by Steve Rodgers, I am well aware of what a unique opportunity it's been to be lead and inspired by someone that lives what they teach. He is a master at authentically inspiring all to achieve beyond levels of complacency or normal. His approach to life and business takes away the ordinary, forcing a new perspective and vision to live into. Go for the Gold"

- Eileen Schwartz, Founder and CEO The Success Table Coaching platform, Certified John Maxwell coach

"This book will speak to anyone who continually strives for their highest good and their own life's purpose. We often have tragedies in our lives that can be both personal or work related. The important thing is to realize how to overcome these tragedies which are obstacles in allowing us to reach our fullest potential. By doing so, we ultimately find ways to turn our own lead into gold. This book and Steve's story will help inspire you to do just that!"

- Daniel j. Daou
  DAOU vineyards & Winery
  Winemaker and co-proprietor, serial entrepreneur

"*Lead to gold* is an inspiring story and journey helping anyone who has had to overcome obstacles. If you are striving to better yourself or your business and want go for your own gold this book is for you! Life is all about transition and transformation and Steve knows that better than most!"

- Rich German, author of Monetize Your Passion, Cofounder the JV Experience. Top coach, Sea Life lover and advocate

Lead to gold is as REAL as it gets...

Steve shares his story from being a successful CEO to becoming a successful Entrepreneur.

In a market where anyone can pretend to be an EXPERT, is refreshing to see The Real Deal.

- Raul Villacis
  CEO Founder The Next Level Experience, Serial Entrepreneur, Speaker, Coach

Introduction

I met Steve Rodgers in 2006 through Marshall Goldsmith. At the time he was President of Prudential California Realty, a Berkshire Hathaway Home Services of America company. He was working with Marshall as his leadership coach. Throughout the years Steve and I have both been avid students of Marshall and his work, and I've watched Steve apply his positive solutions and innovative thinking to challenges that would have stopped others in their tracks. Instead I've watched him turn lemons into lemonade and disasters into miracles. Over and over. He is a remarkable man and my life is enriched by knowing Steve and his family.

When Steve told me he was planning to change his focus to being an entrepreneur, I supported his plans one hundred percent. I see a very clear fit between his unique vision and skillset, and what an entrepreneur needs to become successful. Not only does Steve have the ability to succeed as an entrepreneur, but he has already demonstrated success by applying his own advice in his personal life and professional career. Even under adverse conditions he has found ways to bring out the potential in himself, the people around him, and the situation.

I am delighted to help Steve tell his story in his first book, "*Lead to gold.*" If you're an entrepreneur, you'll find both inspiration and practical advice that can help you weather your own ups and downs as you navigate this territory. When you need a lift, remember Steve's positive spirit, study how he responded to difficulties, and try what he suggests. When you're reviewing your business plans and wondering how to improve profits, cut costs or expand, study his formulas for business success and adapt the appropriate parts to your situation.

Steve has written a terrific companion book for every entrepreneur, and anyone who wants to improve their life or their business.

Enjoy his book!

Marilyn McLeod
Collaborator and Entrepreneur

Lyda Goldsmith, Marilyn McLeod and myself at the book launch party for Marshalls latest NY Times best-selling book Triggers

Marshall Goldsmith and
myself at his home
enjoying a fun party

Foreword by Brian Tracy

All successful people, men and women, are big dreamers. They imagine what their future could be, ideal in every respect, and then they work every day toward their distant vision, that goal or purpose. We all know life is filled with change. There is change by force, by choice or by circumstance. The key in life is how you handle and react to change. Do you fear it and fret over it? Are you creating more worry, stress and negativity in your thinking and in life, or do you embrace change and use it to propel you to all new heights and exciting new places? I know transition in life can be difficult and daunting. It creates many situations in our lives where we can feel out of control and unsure about our futures. It is only human to have these feelings. We all have them and they will always be constant. But is it possible to take the inevitable process of change and transition in business and life and positively redirect it? Can we decide to use it as our secret power and our secret weapon to forge ahead towards our desired dreams? I believe it is and I know you are about to embark on a journey in reading this book "*Lead to gold*" that will help crystallize your thinking. You will appreciate the processes that will show you how this can be done.

I've found that luck is quite predictable. If you want more luck, take more chances. Be more active. Show up more often. Look for guidance from someone who has already demonstrated success in the area where you want to succeed. Steve Rodgers has paid his dues, succeeding more than once both as an entrepreneur and as CEO of a large corporation in California. In addition to his ability to distill his strategy for success into this step-by-step guide for entrepreneurs, he also opens his heart and reveals the foundations underpinning his outward success. The spiritual practices he blends with his diligent attention to his daily tasks also allow him to keep himself and his projects on track.

Steve Rodgers is a longtime friend and associate of mine who has forged his own journey in life doing these very things. Steve shares his story here on the pages ahead in a riveting, honest and transparent display of his own fears, triumphs, success and failures. You will see a man who has had dreams materialized and fulfilled as he followed many of the universal principles I teach and many great leaders and teachers before me have taught. The brilliant Napoleon Hill who wrote "Think and Grow Rich" said, "Anything the mind can conceive and believe it can achieve." I have seen Steve use these principles time and time again in his life. His rise to becoming a Warren Buffett CEO of a Berkshire Hathaway firm was nothing less than amazing. Breaking through his own doubt, fears, insecurities and failures have led him to triumph to countless successes and ultimately find his own inner strength and process to turn Lead into Gold.

The business arena for anyone is challenging in this day and age to say the least. Business is as competitive as ever, especially with the world of an ever changing technology eco system that surrounds us all. This only makes it more exciting and also daunting at the same time. You see in the early days of doing business the market competition was local to your community. There was maybe one butcher, barber, a few retail shops and perhaps a shopping center or two not far away in many of our neighborhoods. But in the last 20 years the world of technology changed all that to make it a more global world than ever before. That has created new challenges and new competition as well as many new opportunities. And the last 5 years have sped things up even faster, forcing businesses to be better than ever, to do it faster, cheaper, with more transparency and while delivering a stellar consumer experience. How in this ever-changing climate of rapid change do you stay true to your dreams, your business and yourself? Can you create a balanced and healthy life filled with success, happiness, fulfillment and a higher purpose that fuels your spirit? You cannot control what happens to you, but you can control your attitude toward what happens to you. You have that power and can choose to follow a plan, your heart, and in that you will be mastering change rather than allowing it to master you.

The analogy of *Lead to gold* is the concept, chemistry and alchemy of turning something useful and good into something even better and more valuable. If you can fathom the idea that the essence of transition and transformation of something as basic as earth's ore and minerals is also possible in our own lives, can any of that really be done? Or is it all hocus pocus and something left up to fate, destiny and the cards you are dealt in life? I challenge you to be bold enough to say yes, this is possible. The formulas for a better, deeper more valuable life is at our finger tips and we do have all the tools necessary to manifest our dreams and create the life we want. Let's not let the never ending hurdles, setbacks and sometimes tragedies of life throw us off course and steal the gold from us that we know is rightfully ours. Keep going, keep reaching, keep taking action and use the principles Steve has learned on his path and references in this book. Incorporate it into your own life. You deserve in your business, in your life and in your biggest unspoken dreams to go for the Gold and make it as real as the lead that may have been holding you down and back. The journey has only just begun! Enjoy it!

Brian Tracy and myself after one of our regular lunches to catch up, share ideas and discuss the big picture ideas of life.

Table of Contents

Introduction

"Control your own destiny or someone else will."
— Jack Welch

Foreword

"And still, after all this time, the Sun has never said
to the Earth, 'You owe me.'
Look what happens with love like that. It lights up
the sky."
— Hāfez

"The individual who says it is not possible should
move out of the way of those doing it."
— Tricia Cunningham

"The only real mistake is the one from which we
learn nothing."
— Henry Ford

Chapter 3: Birth of an Entrepreneur
Pg.90

"There is only one thing that makes a dream
impossible to achieve: the fear of failure."
— Paulo Coelho, The Alchemist

Chapter 4: How to Materialize
the Dream
Pg. 155

"Thomas Edison dreamed of a lamp that could be
operated by electricity, began where he stood to put
his dream into action, and despite more than ten
thousand failures, he stood by that dream until he
made it a physical reality. Practical dreamers do not
quit. "

— Napoleon Hill

Chapter 5: How the Numbers
Fit the Dream
Pg. 179

"I dream my painting and I paint my dream."
— Vincent van Gogh

Chapter 6: Building the Team
Pg. 205

"Remember: Upon the conduct of each depends the fate of all."
— Alexander the Great

Chapter 7: Products and Branding
Pg. 237

"In everyone's life, at some time, our inner fire goes out. It is then burst into flame by an encounter with another human being. We should all be thankful for those people who rekindle the inner spirit."
— Albert Schweitzer

Chapter 8: Marketing and Promotion
Pg. 256

"Only those who will risk going too far can possibly find out how far one can go."
— T. S. Eliot

Chapter 9: The Art of Seduction
Pg. 277

"Negative results are just what I want. They're just as valuable to me as positive results. I can never find the thing that does the job best until I find the ones that don't."
— Thomas A. Edison

Chapter 10: Operations and Infrastructure
Pg. 298

"I believe that people make their own luck by great preparation and good strategy."
— Jack Canfield

Chapter 11: Your Customers: Life or Death
Pg. 322

"The things you do for yourself are gone when you are gone, but the things you do for others remain as your legacy."
— Kalu Ndukwe Kalu

Chapter 12: Higher Power Google Earth
Pg. 349

"I never made one of my discoveries through the process of rational thinking."
— Albert Einstein

Chapter 13: Commitment and the Entrepreneurial Mind
Pg. 379

"Success is stumbling from failure to failure with no loss of enthusiasm."
— Winston S. Churchill

Preface

Thank you for picking up this book or reading it digitally. The intention of this book is to help guide, direct and share stories and situations from my life that may be helpful in your path in your own life.

This book comes from a history of my business and personal life combined with some stories, how-to's and inspiration that I hope will resonate with you.

I have the book blocked out into several sections. In the first section I share with you segments of my business career path and the high's and low's on that journey. You will see from my story that as much as I had many successes along the way, I also had an equal amount of challenges and failures, and in some cases, tragic situations appear. But I took these combined experiences and turned them into my '_Lead to gold_' approach that I'll be sharing with you in this book.

Some middle sections of the book will get into step-by-step how-to's that you need to have in setting up general business models. This book is not intended to be a step-by-step detailed how-to book in setting up all businesses, but simply tying in vision, process and motivation. This, my first book, touches the surface of many things I plan to cover in the future.

The remaining chapters tie in additional inspiration and motivational stories. The entire book will have a spiritual tone throughout, which is what I have come to realize my life is fully about when I am most engaged. This reflects how I live my own life on my path moving forward.

I hope you enjoy this book and understand the process in which I wrote it. My intention is to move forward as a writer, author, speaker and workshop provider and have subsequent books and programs that will dig down much deeper into these individual topics. So you could say that this is kind of an overview in a curriculum of my thinking, my path and my new destiny. I am moving forward with you on my path of ever transitioning, transforming and evolving to my own highest good, as I continue my own process of turning 'Lead into Gold.'

I hope that as you continue on your own path, some of these will resonate with you and they will be of value in your life as well.

You can use the power of transitions, forced or chosen, to your advantage. Learn how to make the unexpected challenges, bumps and hurdles of life become your friend and enhance growth rather than diminish it. Learn that consistent transitions can lead to greater transformations and evolution in your life and business.

This book is about overcoming adversity and forced transitions by turning them into meaningful opportunities. We will explore the paths that you can choose as a transition in life, be it personal or professional, and create a plan that will result in a greater good. Some of the key areas we address will focus around:

- Vision and dreams

- Overcoming fears

- Building a strong base foundation

- Breaking through fear to empowerment

- Daily mindset and rituals

- Higher purpose

We will also explore how spirituality works to fuel your dreams and life purpose.

As someone open to exploring new territory, there are always many questions. Have you ever asked yourself any of the following questions?

<u>As a Business Person</u>

- How do I create a company, form the vision, get the

  courage and articulate the dream?

- How do I find and hire the right team to get things

  off the ground?

- How do I create business plans?

- How do I raise capital?

- How do I find leases and locations (if you're in a

  brick and mortar business)?

- How do I market the business and create presence online?

- How do I create infrastructure that supports my company?

- How do I create a unique customer experience?

- How do I manage all of the things in the process from operations, administration, marketing, technology and training?

- How do I create multiple streams of income for me in my business offering?

- How do I take those ideas and opportunities, and roll it up into a vision that has yet to materialize?

As an Employee

- How do I become more effective in my job and create balance and abundance in my existing workplace?

- If I'm not happy in my current job, how do I transition out into something more that's going to be monetarily safe and also fulfill my new path?

- How do I make the best of a situation in my workplace when I feel that I might be stuck?

- How do I create more harmony in my workplace when I don't feel like I'm supported by others?

- I don't really like my job, but I'm not really sure what I want to do. What can I do next?

- I've been at this job forever. I'm not sure how I could ever leave it. How would I do that?

- I don't feel appreciated in my workplace. I feel like it's the same old thing day after day. How can I find a way to break free?

- I was fired from my job. How am I possibly going to recover from that? I'm not sure what to do.

- I've just quit my job because I was miserable. How do I find my new path to my new higher purpose?

<u>As a Person</u>

- I've just gone through a break-up in a relationship. How do I transition to feeling like I'm happy again?

- I don't feel fulfilled in my relationship. What can I do to create more meaning?

- I sometimes ask myself, "Is there all there is? There has got to be something more."

- I'm having health challenges. How do I find ways to transition and just stay positive and take care of myself?

- I've lost someone who has died. How do I transition and transform through that? There's so much grieving.

- How do I use my unique talents and create the lifestyle I desire?

As a Spiritual Being

- I'm trying to find the right path so that I have a connection to higher meaning and higher purpose in life.

- I don't really have a connection with God, but I'd like to have one.

- I'm kind of turned off by my old faith that I grew up with but how do I change now?

- How do I transition into something with a connection to a higher purpose that feels more meaningful to me?

- How can I be sure of my higher purpose and calling?

- I want to be of service to others and the world at a high level but how do I make that more of a reality?

- I would like to incorporate my spiritual beliefs into more of a daily practice. How do I do that?

'Lead into Gold' is the process of helping people be aware of and understand about transitioning and transforming into something else considered more valuable than what exists now – thus, the phrase '*Lead to gold.*'

My concept of '*Lead to gold*' was inspired by many things. But one of the greatest was a book called The Alchemist by Paulo Coelho, which I have always loved and have re-read many times. In his book Paulo Coelho talks about the journey of a young shepherd boy who goes on a path throughout many lands seeking many answers, treasures and rewards.

The book is a journey about his transition, that through his trials, tribulations and obstacles through the desert, villages and countries on his path, ultimately he finds that the answers were always right within him anyway – not unlike the Wizard of Oz and the phrase, "There is no place like home."

What I take away from some of those phrases, that "there's no place like home" or "the answers are within us" is just that, that we are good enough. We have the answers within us, but we must find different ways to pull them out or to experience them in our existing day to day lives and practice continually to glean the answers. A recap of the premise of the book:

> *A recurring dream troubles Santiago, a young and adventurous Andalusian shepherd. He has the dream every time he sleeps under a sycamore tree that grows out of the ruins of a church. During the dream, a child tells him to seek treasure at the foot of the Egyptian pyramids. Santiago consults a gypsy woman*

to interpret the dream, and to his surprise she tells him to go to Egypt. A strange, magical old man named Melchizedek, who claims to be the King of Salem, echoes the gypsy's advice and tells Santiago that it is his Personal Legend to journey to the pyramids. Melchizedek convinces Santiago to sell his flock and set off to Tangier. When Santiago arrives in Tangier, a thief robs him, forcing him to find work with a local crystal merchant. The conservative and kindly merchant teaches Santiago several lessons, and Santiago encourages the merchant to take risks with his business. The risks pay off, and Santiago becomes a rich man in just a year.

Santiago decides to cash in his earnings and continue pursuing his Personal Legend: to find treasure at the pyramids. He joins a caravan crossing the Sahara Desert toward Egypt and meets an Englishman who is studying to become an alchemist. He learns a lot from the Englishman during the journey. For one, he learns that the secret of alchemy is written on a stone called the Emerald Tablet. The ultimate creation of alchemy is the Master Work, which consists of a solid called the Philosopher's Stone that can turn lead to gold, and a liquid called the Elixir of Life that can cure all ills. Santiago learns the Englishman is traveling with the caravan to the Saharan oasis of Al-Fayoum, where a powerful, 200-year-old alchemist resides. The Englishman plans to ask the alchemist the secret of his trade. And thus the journey with many adventures, life lessons and magical, memorable moments begin. Santiago and those he encounters will never be the same.

SparkNotes Editors. "SparkNote on The Alchemist." SparkNotes.com. SparkNotes LLC. 2010. Web. 5 Mar. 2016.

I was inspired by the theme of the book, The Alchemist. I also love the word 'alchemy.' I realize that I look at my own life being all about transition, transformation and evolution (which I'll share in further chapters in the book with some examples). At least as the stories go, the ancient magical alchemists turned 'Lead into Gold.'

Even though lead has many uses in our day to day lives, lead seems to be perceived as, although valuable, that if it could be turned into gold, it would seem to be even more valuable. Gold seems to be higher in demand, less available and more rare, so it garners a higher price and also can be molded into precious treasures and beautiful jewelry. It also is an indicator in gauging our financial markets.

This concept of helping turn 'Lead into Gold' is a big part of finding happiness in life for me. In our current situation how much do we appreciate what we have to the fullest? Do we experience the lead in our lives as a gift? You may eventually find ways to be your own alchemist and turn what you consider as the lead in your life into gold. I hope this book helps you in that journey.

This concept of turning 'Lead into Gold' led me to thinking about my new consulting company which I started this past year. I felt so strongly about it that I used the word 'alchemy' in my business name. My company's new name is called Alchemy Advisors, which is a consulting, coaching, training and education firm. The slogan is "Helping people transition, transform and evolve to their highest good."

As you read this book you'll learn more about my story. I knew instinctively that I would have to do just that, to turn the lead in my life that was holding me back, into new opportunities and vision that would allow me to move forward in a productive and positive way. I had already achieved my large vision of becoming the CEO of a company. I then started and ran my own business as successful entrepreneur. I had set a target. I had set out on a mission. And then I backed into it. But next I had to take action. You will see how I use visualization to help me:

When you embark on the goal of attaining a big dream, you might take on something bigger than yourself. You might not have a clue as to how to achieve your goal, or if it will even work out. The Universe and Mother Nature will conspire towards your success. The Universe will bring people, places, and things to you that allow your dream to digest and/or materialize. It does not mean you do not have to plan. You do. You will need to plan, you will need to focus, you will need to execute, and you will need to take action. You will need to be fearless in your faith with due diligence every day towards your dream, your vision, and your idea. You will need to strike and strike again! This is whether your dream is building a business, a new job, writing a book, buying a business, creating a new idea, getting a patent, breaking away from your company, creating a new company, doing something online, becoming an artist, becoming a musician, being a teacher, getting married or even becoming the President of the United States. Whatever your dream is, it is out there and it is possible if you choose to do what it takes to make it real.

I encourage you to live big, to dream big, and to create your 'have-to,' your 'want-to' and your 'why' into one collective consciousness within yourself. It has to be in your whole being: body, mind and soul, every day. This book will encourage you, teach you, and guide you through the steps of breaking through your fears. It's intended to help you delve into your passion, and create the systems, processes, steps and procedures to turn that dream into a reality. Let's get started!

Chapter **1**
CEO Story

ം

      Today seems like any other day. As the alarm goes off, I wake and look at the sun streaming through the window. I roll out of bed, put my feet on the floor and realize this is not like any other day. As I do every day, I go to my bathroom and look in the mirror. While brushing my teeth and getting ready to shave, I stare at myself six inches from the mirror. I say to myself with amazement, "Wow, I really am the CEO today. It finally happened. It has come true." My face is joyous and happy like the face of a kid on Christmas morning. After many years of hard work, planning, affirmations, belief and persistence, I'm actually stepping in as the CEO of a multi-billion dollar sales volume real estate company.

I had started at Prudential California Realty in 1994 as a branch real estate manager. I knew even then I had a vision for more, and I had a feeling my vehicle to get there would be this company. I had a feeling it was going to allow me the path to make that happen, so I set out to make my vision a reality. In 2006 I became the CEO of not only Prudential California Realty, but also a company that was owned by Warren Buffett, a Berkshire Hathaway Home Services of America company.

Originally my desire was to be the very, very best manager that I could be and make a huge name for myself by making a difference and creating value. I knew this would lead to the next opportunity, and that is exactly what happened. One of the first offices I managed was one that had been taken over from Merrill Lynch by Prudential. Merrill Lynch used to be in the real estate business, but most know it in the investment and insurance world. At the point they decided to get out of the real estate business is the time Prudential got even deeper into the real estate space. Prudential bought Merrill Lynch and converted all of their existing real estate locations to Prudential real estate offices. The owners of the Prudential franchise in San Diego was able to pick up numerous offices in that marketplace, which was big news. However, many of the Merrill Lynch real estate agents had fled and gone to other locations during this changing, turbulent time for the company.

One of the offices I took over was in the inland area of San Diego County called Rancho Bernardo. In the Merrill Lynch days, it had been a flourishing office, but when I stepped in some time later and took it over as a manager, it was the low office on the totem pole. It was losing money, it had lost a lot of agents, its reputation had been tarnished, and it was in a sad state of affairs. I stepped into that office intending to find someone who could help me manage the office so I could fix the problem. I was in a newly floating catch-all manager position at the time. After looking at about 60 candidates, my gut told me that the very best thing I could do was to take over that office and build it myself. The owners came to the conclusion at about the same time.

My mission in this new consultant role coming into the company was to manage the office and then find someone who could fix it permanently. In a short amount of time I had become fond of the people in that office. I was amazed by the heart and loyalty of the people who were still left there as supporters. Instead of being mad at the people who left and hadn't supported the dream of building this company, I decided to focus on the people who were still there and wanting to make a difference. I see this as a big lesson in life. When we have had losses or people have abandoned us, or we feel like we have not gotten something we deserved and it's not fair, that is not fun. It is not a great feeling, but it is also important to focus on the things that we do have, the breaks that we have been given, and all of the many gifts that surround us now in the form of people, places or things. I chose to do that in this particular scenario.

From there I took control of that office, and with my team we turned it around. Within 2-3 years we had transformed it from a losing branch to a branch that was making a lot of profit. A few more years after that it became one of the top ten offices for the Prudential Company on a national level. I was very proud to be on the convention stage, representing that office in front of thousands of people at a Prudential Real Estate Conference, receiving the plaque and the trophies for being in the top ten, and sometimes the top five, in sales volume and in units throughout the country. People in the crowd were cheering. Many of our office team members had come to the convention, but also thousands of people that I didn't know were also cheering. I felt honored and proud of the achievements we had accomplished together. I knew that much was possible, and I also knew that it was possible to take it to a whole new level. Following that path led to many, many more years of success, and that success led to opening more offices and growing our team. I became a regional manager, a general manager, then President, COO and ultimately CEO.

It had been a fifteen year run, not an overnight success. I had to re-duplicate that same experience many, many times. I would go to the next project or the next office and apply the same tools I had previously used with great success. Getting committed, finding out about the team around me, figuring out what I had and didn't have, and deciding on what I needed to create dictated the steps necessary to make it happen. It was usually about getting a great team behind me and making sure I had systems and processes in place that allow me to achieve what I want to achieve. Then, it is getting up and doing the daily hard work of the activities, which I call the big rock items.

In most companies, anybody who is at the high executive or CEO level is there to generate profits and create a better experience with the consumer. It is about making sure that the people around them are doing the activities which cause this to happen. One of the main tasks a manager does in a real estate business is to recruit outside talent. The business needs other talented sales people or individuals who can help make contributions to the company and drive revenue. I became very, very good at that. I had a great tenacity for recruiting and steering talent to our company. It was fun and enjoyable, but a long and arduous process that takes a lot of courting, wooing and persistence. It creates a lot of momentum because one great person and one great thing leads to another. This all added up to a lot of great successes along the way over my years with the company. When I started with Prudential as part of a team we had about ten offices, and over the years that I worked for them I am proud to say that we, as a group and as a team, opened up another almost 100 offices throughout all of southern California.

This means we re-duplicated the process many times over the years. My influence was present, but it was a team effort at Prudential. It always is, but I had a big part in the momentum and creating things that were possible within that organization. The two owners had great drive, talent and passion, and that helped set the tone and path for everyone.

There were many trials and tribulations, successes, ups and downs, and many stories in between that got me to this place: I had become a CEO. And all of this for a guy who barely graduated from high school and never finished college. I had actually made the effort, but after two or three years of going to community college with only four or five semesters to show for it, I realized that institutional education was probably not my path. I would not be an academic or even have a college degree. So I looked for other paths to success, first in the restaurant and hospitality business, and then ultimately in real estate. I wanted to prove to myself that I could become a success. I wanted to prove that I could become an entrepreneur, and I could become wealthy without a college degree. This was a major breakthrough for me in thinking of new possibilities. When you first don't find a clear and valued path, create a new one!

Back to my first day as the new CEO, I finished shaving and nodded my head in approval for this milestone in my life, gratefully and truly. It was the first day of the rest of my life as I always say. I put on my suit, fixed the perfect purple tie for this momentous day, and made sure my shoes where shiny bright. As I kissed my wife Mary Lou goodbye, we shared knowing, proud smiles. We had made it through. With twinkles sparkling in our eyes, we began our day. We knew that this was something I had wanted and had worked hard to achieve for years.

There had been so many times in the previous years when Mary Lou shared her frustration about the company and the owners when they did not deliver on what was promised. "Why don't you just quit already?!" was asked more than once. On this day it all came together and it was clear why I had not. She then smiled and kissed me once more and sent me off into the world with my driver, Tony, waiting below. The day was looking brighter, clearer and even more promising than the day before.

Tony and Vanilla Lattes

For the past year or so I had been blessed with a car and driver. The car was a necessity and luxury all rolled into one. Since my responsibility with Prudential covered all of Southern California, with more than a hundred real estate offices spanning miles and miles of SoCal freeways, having a driver was essential. It was a gift to have someone drive while I spoke on the phone and viewed emails on my laptop. There were also the little perks of having Starbucks in the car waiting with a newspaper in the morning. I won't lie; that tall skinny sugar free vanilla latte was always a treasured treat. And I'll admit it was a nice stroke for the ego pulling up somewhere with a driver.

My driver Tony was a spry, fit ex-pilot and boxer who always had a kind word and a positive attitude. He had gray hair and was suave-looking but also had a slight, hard, long - lived edge. He had surely lived and seen life at many different levels. Tony always brightened my day and it was a real pleasure to work with him over the years.

As I got in the car that morning, I prepared myself mentally and enjoyed the ride even more than usual. I had been going to this same corporate office for years, but today was different. Today I was going to the large corner office of the CEO, and that office would be mine. Tony dropped me off at the front door, handed my briefcase to me, and said, "Mr. Rodgers, go get 'em. I'm proud of ya!" Tony, with a steel positive look in his eye and a sense of great wisdom, told me to stick to my guns, be tough, and stay true to myself. I thanked him, knowing this was great advice.

I left the elevator and greeted Susan at the front desk and smiled. With a wink she said, "Congratulations, Mr. Rodgers!" I thanked her and walked into the corporate headquarters, nodded, greeted, welcomed and spoke to each staff member along the way. They all knew there would be a staff meeting later that day where I would offer a full expression of the vision and the path we would be taking. My heart was swelling, and my pride was at an all-time high. I felt as though I was in a dream. But this dream was real, and I knew I had created it. I was clearly in the moment relishing and deeply valuing the day, and truly looking forward to the process I knew was before me.

I arrived in my office and went to sit behind the desk. This was where the previous CEO had sat for years. I had sat across from her many times talking with her regarding reports, numbers, and getting decisions; talking about acquisitions and mergers; talking about management issues, challenges, problems and hiring talent. But I had never sat in 'the' chair. Beyond my new job responsibilities, I was looking forward to that great view from the floor to ceiling glass windows on every side of that exquisite corner office.

I put down my briefcase and walked around the office and noticed how bare it was from my previous visit there, my last meeting with the former CEO. I knew I would be moving my things in and creating my own space. I had already planned what colors, pictures and items I would bring in to make it my own. With great anticipation I slowly sat down in the chair, knowing that I would have just a few minutes to myself before I launched into the day that I knew would not end, and would be continuous from morning 'til night. But first I took in these moments while sitting in the chair. I swiveled in it and looked around. I looked out the window. I was smiling from ear to ear.

While reveling in a feeling of such great pride, such great honor and appreciation, something inside of me loudly said, "This still isn't it." And I thought, "Who's saying that?" I looked around, I looked over my shoulder, I looked out the window, and it said it again, "This still isn't it." I suddenly felt my enthusiasm deflate. The pride that I was feeling, the enthusiasm that had been emanating from me – all of a sudden it all took a dip. It was almost like the sudden drop after the sugar rush from eating a candy bar when within hours, your blood sugar takes a nosedive. This feeling was deep in my soul, deep in my stomach. I had believed that the many long years of hard work would bring me to this important pinnacle. I had planned to be in this spot for many, many years to come. I knew I would feel proud and make it my own unique journey. But now something in this moment was so clear and so profound that I knew somehow my plans were not to be. Something inside of me said, "This will be two to three years at the most, then you will have finished what you came here to do and you will be moving on. This is not your final destination."

As much as I knew this was true and real, there was also a sense of sadness around it. The dream I had fought for and looked forward to for so long suddenly seemed to be taken away from me. But instead of reflecting on this further, I quickly swiveled around in my new chair, turned on my computer, and feverishly got on with prepping and planning the day. I began to check emails, daily reports and my calendar for the day. I glossed over that feeling of deflation and swept it away as quickly as it had come. The day was calling my name and there was so much to be done.

I ended up staying in that position of CEO until December of 2008. During my CEO journey there were many, many business and life lessons learned. I have real scars to prove it. But the lessons were deep and involved. Did I say that diplomatically enough? Do you hear the cost of wisdom learned? Do you hear my ultimate valuing of the gifts that came from those challenges? It was a tough road, it's true. Would I do it again? I wouldn't want to go through some of the painful parts of those years again. But I do know everything happens for a reason, and there is ultimately a gift when the smoke clears.

The Road to CEO

I had many obstacles to overcome and a massive amount of corporate politics to maneuver through. The days and months were long in part due to a declining real estate market and falling home prices.

I didn't start out as a CEO. I started out as a salesperson who had a desire to help people, and to grow. I wanted to build the best practice I could, and that is exactly what I did. I enjoyed sales, but I was aware of a yearning and something calling inside of me for leadership. I had been in leadership ten years prior in the hotel/restaurant industry. Many leadership skills are adaptable from one industry to another. I took several of those skills including the ability to inspire and motivate people, and helping people learn skills and techniques that would help them feel more confident. I would learn to do something myself, then I would translate, educate and train others to be able to do those very same things.

My philosophy was to bring my best. Whether I was a waiter, bartender, manager, coordinating banquets, working comedy clubs, or dinner theatres, I put my head and heart into my role. I made sure that I learned from mentors and other people around me, and I excelled at what I did. I always carried out my role with more enthusiasm, more energy, more excitement, and more commitment. I was hungry to make a difference, to be noticed, and to make sure that I was being of value to others. I always had a very high drive. I had something higher than myself calling me to something greater. I knew from a very young age that I wanted to do something great with my life. I realized that everything was a stepping stone to something else. I knew somehow that I couldn't get to the next place without fully experiencing gratitude in each moment during my life process.

There have been many times in my life, and especially in my early days, that I didn't enjoy the conditions in which I found myself. There were years when I struggled to pay the electric bill, and rolled quarters to get gas so I could get myself to work. At times I worked three jobs, taking a bus between jobs because I didn't have a car. But I was still always a happy person. I was always focused on the thought that maybe this was not the most fortunate situation, but it was temporary and it could be changed. I always believed, and still believe, that we always have a choice. How we look at any situation and how we view the world is always our own choice. We have the power to choose what we can do to make a difference in each moment, in each situation and in each day.

Nothing is permanent. Everything changes. When I was waiting tables, when I was in low-paying jobs, or when I was in positions that I didn't want, I knew that this too would pass. I knew that I had to make the effort to learn from what I was experiencing in those moments. I had to make the biggest contribution that I could possibly make. I had to create the biggest difference that I could. In my mind this allowed me the right to be worthy, to show that I had the skill, that I had the stamina, and that I had the desire and ability to be able to go to that next level. There were many times in the early days even before real estate that this attitude and work ethic led to me being promoted from a waiter job to an assistant manager or a manager position. It also led to going from one restaurant store to another store, or taking on larger locations with more opportunity.

As I reflect on the ambition I had, I believe I had a CEO mindset from a very young age. I've always looked at the bigger picture. I saw the world in a visionary way about what was possible the next month, the next year, and the next three years. I had high ambitions about how I could start materializing to make that happen. Looking at the bigger picture is an important part of any person being a CEO in their own company, the CEO of a large company, or even their own life. I always say we are the CEOs of our own lives, so make the decisions and choices that will serve you best. You are the one holding the vision for everyone else to follow. You hold this clearly for yourself so that other people can believe, perceive or contemplate. How do you paint that picture with thoughts, words, actions, deeds and activities that allow people to feel your vision is possible? How do you keep them on board with a sense of enthusiasm that you are getting there? This is sometimes a stepping stone process, and together you and your team can make those things happen.

I used that same thinking in my jobs. I would think about what I wanted to do next in my life, and what kind of actions or steps I would have to take to get there. At various times I focused on learning better skills, treating people with more respect, working harder, working smarter or making sure that I was of greater value to others. All of those factors in my thinking, words and actions were the reality that created the next opportunity to arise. I always made sure that I was the best at what I could do in that time period. When I eventually became the CEO of a company, I made sure that I dressed up and I showed up. I did the work with passion and I did it with heart. I kept a bigger picture in mind about what I had envisioned for that particular company and did things to reflect that in some way every day.

When I stepped into the CEO role of Prudential it was the fifth largest real estate company in the United States, so it was already materializing a pretty big vision internally and externally. But I had an even bigger vision about the possibilities of where that company could go. So although I was a CEO who had risen up the food chain, I rose through the food chain and helped keep the company vision along the way. Getting to that higher level is a long process but at each level you need to find ways to add value regardless of your current level. Helping sell the vision is key in any role.

Worthy of Success

Another key point is that I also believed I was worthy. Anything you are doing in life, whether you are running a business, in sales, an executive, consulting, or an employee in a company looking for better opportunities, you first need to start with the belief and the mindset that you are worthy of your success, that you are worthy of that position. You may not have the skills, the technique or the technical ability yet, but you have to believe in the worthiness of the opportunities that could and should exist for you. You matter! You have to believe that you're capable of doing what it takes to create opportunities within your life. You have to be clear about what you would do to make someone else's life better if you had those opportunities.

I always believed that I was worthy. Even though I grew up as a fat kid I had very strong confidence at a very young age. I was picked on and bullied in school and in the neighborhood. As a fat kid and I was even picked on by my four other brothers. I came from a family of five boys and believe me, the harassment, the bullying, and the feeling alone, feeling "less than" were not fun. I was pounded on from right inside my own family by my brothers. Eventually the pressure from schoolmates, neighborhood kids, and actually the world in general, caused me to escape into food. I gained even more weight and more fat as I numbed my feelings. We are all human and we all have frailties, and we may often turn to food, alcohol, drugs or other addictions to try to eliminate our pain. Everyone has some kind of escape they've developed which is sometimes healthy and sometimes not healthy. For me it was a food addiction at a young age and probably not so healthy. I can now say I am in the best health of my life. I don't smoke, drink and have been a vegan for a year. I exercise daily. But this was a long time process to achieve.

I have many reasons why I could conclude that I'm "not supposed to be worthy." I did not graduate college. I did not come from a really strong, well-educated family. I came from a great family with a great work ethic, but I didn't come from a highly educated, college- oriented family, and I didn't come from money. We were a family in the Navy so I moved around a lot as I grew up. I didn't have roots anywhere for long, but I always had a strong connection to family and the foundation that they set. Something inside of me knew I was always worthy. I was worthy to my Higher Power and I was worthy to my parents. I was worthy to myself, and that sense of worthiness really helped me as I grew from becoming a kid to a young adult, and then to an adult. I carried that sense of worthiness and I still do to this day. In hindsight, I believe this stemmed from my strong spiritual base which I developed at a young age with the base help of my parents.

If you feel that you are worthy, then you feel that you have the right to seek out and become anything you want in life. If you want to become CEO of a company or anything else, you can create the path and any desire to make your dreams happen in your life. I found this out many times in my life, like when I had the opportunity to meet people like Mr. Warren Buffet and many other noteworthy leaders. I felt I was worthy to be in the same room, at a cocktail party or a dinner with them. I did not feel out of place, I did not feel awkward, nor did I feel that I wasn't anything but deserving of being there. I felt that I brought value, whether it was in my energy, my outlook, or what I had accomplished, and what I still had to learn. I always ask lots of questions of others more successful than I am. If you are giving value to people and you are making a contribution to the world around you, this also creates a sense of worthiness.

On the path of creating this life, there were many times as the CEO I tried to reflect and carry that memory I had of how hard the path to climb the corporate ladder had been as I persisted. I considered how I could carry that message to inspire other people around me. When I saw other people who weren't feeling worthy, or if I could tell that people had low self-confidence, I knew those people were not living up to their highest and best purpose or place. I would use my memories and stories of my own path to see if I could help them along their path. I might do this through communicating, consulting, coaching, group talks, pats on the back, kind words and kicks in the butt - whatever it would take. I would use skills I had learned to help nurture and bring along other people who I knew who could not only contribute to their own lives by making a difference and letting their worthiness be shown, but that their actions and their improvement in their contribution would make a better company and a better environment for others.

Golden Nuggets

 Diligent, consistent, focused effort towards a goal can result in great achievements.

 We shape the results of our efforts according to our choices along the way.

 As the leader of your project and your life, you are holding the vision for everyone else to follow.

 Decide you are worthy of the success you desire!

Chapter *2*
Berkshire and Life's Big Lessons

Being part of a Berkshire Hathaway company definitely gave me many moments of deep pride and prestige that I will never forget. It was one of the highlights of my business career to date, and the icing on the cake were the numerous times I was able to meet Mr. Warren Buffett. Being an executive within the network provided me with numerous opportunities to see Mr. Buffett in various group business settings, dinners, and Berkshire Hathaway shareholder conferences. Warren is like a financial rockstar. If you have ever been to a Berkshire Hathaway shareholder conference, you will know what I mean.

At any one time, shareholder conferences might have 50, 100 or even a 1,000 people at the meetings. This is not typical and different for the caliber of an organization like Berkshire Hathaway. Berkshire Hathaway shareholder meetings are like a rock concert that lasts a few days. People are wrapped around the building, waiting in line to get into the Quest Center in Omaha. More than 20,000 people attend to see Charlie Munger and Warren Buffett work their magic, which is something to behold. To sit in an audience of 20,000 people with the likes of Bill Gates, millionaires, billionaires and many more wealthy businessmen and women, is amazing. You sit amongst the masses in the audience listening to the financial gurus start the day's show. The crowd consists of business people, investors, wannabe investors, the public and the press, all hanging onto every word that Mr. Buffett says. It is electric.

It becomes a comedy act with Charlie Munger and Warren Buffett. Charlie Munger seems to me like a Mr. Magoo-type cartoon character with great wisdom and insight who pulls no punches. Warren Buffett is the complete financial genius with optimism for a better world. His democratic views and his opinions of society and wealth are controversial at times to say the least. It's amazing that so many dichotomies fit into one man and with such diversity and odd style. It is fascinating to behold as they chew on their See's candies and drink Cherry Cokes, and talk about the many companies that they own, including GEICO, Fruit of the Loom, See's Candy, Dairy Queen, AIG and so many more. Munger and Buffett can answer any question an audience member might have about each of these companies. It is simply fascinating to watch and listen to them.

"Mr. Buffett, how do you view the challenge with Social Security?"

"Mr. Munger, what do you think is going to happen in the stock market this month with the challenge of oil prices?"

"Mr. Buffett, can you tell me how you feel about the insurance industry and the regulations that have been thrown upon them this year?"

"Mr. Buffett, can you tell us why you still live in the same home?"

"Mr. Buffett, can you tell us what you believe the President will do this year on financial issues related to real estate and capital gains?"

These questions fly for hours from an audience of 20,000 with microphones set up in the rows and upper nose bleed rafters. Warren and Charlie simply bat the answers back to the audience like they were hitting ground balls out to third base and sometimes homeruns.

I've repeatedly felt a great sense of pride having been a part of this organization. I have been greatly influenced by the prestige and immense knowledge from many of its key executives. I never reported directly to Warren Buffett, nor would I say by any stretch of the imagination that I had a personal relationship with him. But I did have the honor of meeting this man and felt privileged to be working for his companies. I met him on numerous occasions, had various conversations with him, and it was truly a business career highlight to meet him all the times that I did.

Warren Buffet and myself at one of our many company leadership events."

Adult Musical Chairs

Under that structure, as with many corporate America companies, there are other realities of the day to day business that don't quite fit in line with what is being touted at the top. I am sure many of you have experienced this in your own business dealings, or in your own corporate environments. There are always politics and what I call "adult musical chairs." When businesses are growing and corporations are making money, people are getting raises, companies are being acquired, businesses are being tucked in, profits and numbers are being exceeded, and projections are being broken through. It is a good ride. Due to business growth, you will always need to re-forecast. When things are going gangbusters you might have to re-forecast every month because business is going so well in the real estate space.

However, when the tide turns, as it did it in the real estate market in 2005, and the upward momentum starts to slide downward, no one ever imagines how quickly things can go downhill for an industry, for a company, or for an individual. I can clearly tell you from personal experience that it is no fun going from making multi millions of dollars in profits to experiencing losses. The atmosphere changes quickly and dramatically. It becomes a cut, cut, cut mentality and the musical chairs begin. My first course of action as CEO in 2006 was to keep the Titanic from sinking. I was stepping into a spot with a company that was barely making money although it had made millions and millions the years before. I knew I was definitely ready and I was up for the challenge. I knew it was going to be a rocky road ahead. I just had no idea how rocky!

Finding Heart in a Tough Situation

As a new CEO I needed to prepare a plan of stabilization and recovery. I submitted it to my higher-ups, thinking I was being very lofty in proposing that we close 35 of our 105 offices, slash payroll cost and, unfortunately, also cut talent. The plan was to pull out of markets that we had pursued with heart and that had taken us years to get into. But I knew they wanted a bold approach, and that I had to make those tough decisions. After agonizing about the situation and wrapping my head around it, I put forth a plan with great gusto and enthusiasm. The response that came back was, "Well, okay plan, but we wanted you to close 50."

I thought, "Fifty! You want me to close 50 of 105 offices that we have? Are you kidding me? Do you know how long it took us to grow these offices and to build this company? What happened to 'when things get tough, you're really going to appreciate Warren Buffett'? When the company sold to Berkshire Hathaway in 2001, we were told, 'You're going to be really glad you have Berkshire Hathaway money behind you and the strength of Berkshire Hathaway. That's when it will come true and clear as to why the company was sold'?"

Well, that certainly never came to pass during this period. Those past promises were now long gone like a train that was missed an hour ago. One of my biggest fears when we were sold to a corporate giant was now coming true. Even worse, I was the one leading the march. I knew this was one approach that had worked with many businesses and industries over the years in declining markets. It just was not the approach I fully agreed with or endorsed.

I had come up in the beginning days of this company when we took the "entrepreneurial approach" to expansion. My predecessor and mentor Steve Games, who founded and built this company and eventually sold it to Warren Buffett, had always promoted growth in a tough market. He also believed when everyone else is retreating (as now so many were doing), you grow, build and acquire. It seemed like a plan that had worked famously well before when we hit several "bad markets" over the years. But this time, in this market and with this company, that was not the course to be taken at all. Far from it!

Although my higher ups didn't like my 35 office closure plan and they wanted 50, my response back was, "Well, let's start with the 35 and we'll go from there." The work began and over the next few years, my executive team and I went forward and did just that. There were harsh, harsh decisions to be made about laying people off, letting managers go who had worked with us for years, and pulling out of markets that we had spent years getting into to find the right lease. The time spent to find the right leaders, the right salespeople, to now suddenly rip them out, close them down and call it a day was defeating. It just all seemed so empty, so heartless, and so counter intuitive from our previous 20-year history of proven success. But this was the expected course based on a sliding economy in the real estate world. We soon were to find out this would be one of the worst extended markets in history. The day-to-day grind of dismantling and working hard to also stabilize a company became my daily existence.

There were too numerous heart-wrenching stories to count that happened along the way when we were laying people off and closing offices and divisions. I had to face so many tears and anger from others when they discovered their fate. It was always so brutal to have those conversations. But I made sure when appropriate that I was part of the difficult conversations. I just felt as though I owed it to them, after earning their trust over our years of building the business together, to look them in the eye and tell them like it was, no matter how hard it was and how bad it hurt them and me. I only survived through these long months because I was focused on my strong spiritual belief that everything happens for a reason. I had to believe that this change was releasing them off to a new path that would create great new things for them and their families. Sometimes that happened and, sad to say, sometimes it didn't, at least on the surface. Time then marched on and the company became smaller and smaller.

Rainy Day in California

In December of 2008 I had been waiting for a meeting with the COO of Home Service of America, a Berkshire Hathaway Company, to come out and tour our remaining offices that still existed in Southern California. This was his first visit since being newly appointed to his current position in this world of musical chairs, and in the growth of Berkshire Hathaway. During the decline, certain people made it and certain people did not. Some did rise. He was one of those who rose. It was interesting in retrospect to analyze who, how and why the musical chairs moved around, but for now it just was what it was. I was very excited to have him come out and tour. He was to be here for three days, tour the market, meet all the managers, and have a great heart-to-heart with me about the future of our industry and our marketplace.

I knew when I woke up on this particular December morning, and noticed it was raining cats and dogs, that something felt off and was not shining bright, and it was not just the sun. I also suspected another sign the day before when my car was supposed to have been completed and out of the shop, but it was delayed, and I had to keep the loaner car for another day. I had hoped to have my own car ready for touring my boss. I thought maybe this was going to be a challenging day. For some reason I just had a bad gut feeling. I was normally used to full, challenging days, week after week, and I was experiencing increasing workload and dwindling support. Tony, my driver, was one of the recent casualties. I no longer had him as a driver or his positive smiling face to begin each day. I sure could have used him on this day!

I was driving myself. The plan was for me to pick up this arriving COO from the airport in Orange County. Because of the unusual Southern California rain, the plane had been delayed. My right-hand guy, Tom, my Vice President, said that he would pick them up since he lived in Orange County. I went on with my day, working in the office and keeping myself busy with projects, calls and emails. As the day went on and I received either no answer or odd answers to my calls for an update, I began to feel that something didn't seem right. Finally, in the late afternoon my VP Tom arrived at the San Diego headquarters. When he walked in the office without the other parties I said, "Well, where is he? I thought you were picking him up and you were with them all day."

He said, "I was, but he wanted to stop at the hotel first and clean up. He wanted to know if you could pick him up over there."

My gut said, "Something sounds fishy here."

I looked at Tom and said, "Tom, how did the day go and what did he have to say?"

He gave me some generic basic answers. I asked, "Is there anything else I need to know about here? Anything that's going on? Anything that's weird? What was his mood? What did he ask about? What was the situation?"

He said, "No, everything's good." He slapped me on the back and said, "Good luck. I'm sure you'll get all caught up with him soon. See ya back here."

I was told to call him when I arrived at the hotel, and he would meet me either in the lobby or outside. At first I sat waiting in the rain in my loaner car and realized no one was outside. I asked the valet, "Could you hold my car here? I'm just going to run into the lobby for a minute; they probably are sitting inside."

When I got inside the hotel, there was nobody there. The lobby was empty. I went to the front desk of this pretty nice hotel and asked them if they had seen any gentlemen that were looking around in the last 15 minutes in the lobby. They said, "No."

I described who he was and gave his name. They said, "Oh yes, they checked in about an hour ago, but we haven't seen them come down yet." I heard 'they' and thought "Hmmm, I wonder who else is here." Then my next thought, "Oh, I bet I know," and had even more of a gut sinking feeling.

So I said, "Can you please call their room?"

They called Stan's room and he answered the phone and said, "Oh, hey Steve. Hey can you come up to my room? I'm in 537."

I said, "You want me to come to your hotel room? That's kind of odd."

He said, "Yeah, just come up. We're not quite ready yet."

As I arrived on the fifth floor and left the elevator, I saw Stan standing in the hallway. I had met Stan previously in Omaha and Minnesota, but had never met him in Southern California. He reminded me of a typical engineer/school teacher type of executive that might have a pencil protector in his pocket. As I got off the elevator he was there to greet me, and he said, "Oh, hello Steve."

I looked at him and knew instantly something was odd and said, "Hello, Stan."

He said, "Well just follow me down the hallway."

As I walked down the hallway, my mind was racing a mile a minute with various scenarios, none of them good or with a positive outcome. As he opened the door to his room, I saw another man standing inside. His name was Harold, the HR Director. Harold reminded me of the actor Anthony Hopkins and the character he played in *Silence of the Lambs*, Doctor Hannibal Lecter. I had at this point had numerous meetings and interactions with him due to all the people we had let go over the years. He was sitting at what I remember to be like a card table that was set up in the corner of the room with a few chairs and papers on the table. I thought this was really weird. My gut instantly knew in that second that my path and my life would never be the same again. He stood up and said, "Hello, Steve." I just looked him. I'm not sure what I actually said, but I know what I was thinking.

As they started to sit down in these chairs they invited me to sit down. The whole thing was surreal and in a total awkward engagement of conversation, I said, "What's going on here, guys?"

And they said, "Well, we're here to talk about your future. Sit down."

I said, "It doesn't look to me like there's much of a future here for me for some reason."

They said, "Please sit down."

I said, "No, I think I'd rather stand. I don't think this is going to be a very long meeting." Since I myself had been chopping heads, laying people off, cutting expenses, and firing people left and right for the last two years, I knew what was before me. They went on to explain that we all knew the market was tough and things had really slid down. They talked about California having some of the biggest drops in the country. These were Midwestern men where the market has few highs and lows. They said that my entrepreneurial approach and bucking the system didn't always align with their approach and vision about where they were going. Their focus was different from mine. They had decided it was time to make a change.

"Ah, okay, I get it. You don't want me here anymore. I get it." I added, "So you mean my 15 years of service, helping to build this company and then leading the march on closing 35 offices (versus the 50 they wanted) is just not enough for you." I briefly reminded them of all I had done over the years and also asked how they could do this with no adequate and fair warning. This was such a completely different approach to the way I'd let people go. I guess trying to keep people's jobs and opportunities before them was not the path they wanted to take. Thus in that moment they asked me to sign some papers. They asked me to fill out some documentation. Then they told me I could stay on in a consulting, speaking or teaching role. They said maybe that we could say that I was pursuing other opportunities, or that I was going to look at my other career opportunities and that I was stepping aside. They gave me three or four different options to help me 'save face.'

I said, "Guys, let's not go through that whole drill. Let's call a spade a spade. You want me fired, you don't want me here, and you don't want me at your party, that's fine. I don't want to be at a party where I am not wanted and appreciated. I do not need to lead or even be part of a company that doesn't want me here, so let's call it a day. I will have my attorney look at these documents and I'll contact you. No, I am not signing anything today." I knew that severance packages, terms, legal discussions on many levels were still looming ahead. I was not committing to anything today in any way.

With that I excused myself from the room. As I walked out of the hotel room and looked at the doors sliding open in the elevator, I stepped in. I looked at the glass mirror wall in the elevator and said, "I am no longer the CEO today". Just as I had looked in the bathroom mirror years earlier when I had been brushing my teeth and I knew I was a CEO that day, today was the end of that journey. As I was going down the elevator a bit numb, I thought this was very ironic and I said again, "Wow, I'm no longer the CEO today". I had to laugh a bit out loud and just take that in. There was in that moment a small sense of relief and also a profound but clear higher calling that ran through me. I had no fear, no doubt. I knew this road had come to an end. I then moved into a sense of excitement and euphoria that I didn't expect or would have anticipated if I ever thought that moment might come. All this transpired by the time the elevator doors opened.

When I got down to my car and the valet guy, all of which I had forgotten about, the valet was still letting my car run, sitting in the rain. My briefcase, laptop and belongings were still sitting in the backseat of my car and I hoped everything was there as I had left it. As I ran to my car trying to hold my jacket over my head to stay dry, I heard someone behind me saying, "Steve, Steve." It was Stan with his coat over his head, too. While we stood in the rain, he said that he needed to confiscate my laptop and my Blackberry, because they were company property and contained company information. Stan said that someone would be meeting me back at the corporate office in a few hours so I could clear out my things. I said, "You want my phone and my computer now? What, is this like giving you my badge and my gun and put it on the table, and the sheriff's thrown out of town now? Is that how this works?" I guess I should have known clearly the drill by now as I had been on the other end dishing it out for some time now.

I gave him my cell phone. I said I didn't have my laptop with me. I knew I wanted to copy personal necessary data valuable to me. I didn't say goodbye. I just got in my car and I realized, wow, this is so surreal. This is totally surreal. There was a sense of numbness, shock, and there was also a sense of excitement. I realized in that moment that I should call my wife Mary Lou and fill her in. That was not going to be an easy call. Mary Lou, whom I love with all my heart and who is so many wonderful things in my life, is not the calmest person. She is, as they say, a bit dramatic and wears her heart on her sleeve. This call would stir all of that and more in her. Ready to face her response I reached for my phone, and realized that I couldn't even make a phone call. My phone had just been taken. My own car was in the shop, so the normal car phone that I would have had with a handless speaker was not available. I quickly realized, "Wow, I'm going to have to go to a pay phone."

Up for a Big Adventure

As I drove the car to find a pay phone, I thought, "I don't think I've used a pay phone in five years. Do they even still make pay phones?" I figured I'd better find out. I found a corner AM/PM store and saw in the far corner a pay phone. Wow, they still make them. I pulled my car up to the phone, with it still pouring cats and dogs, and I got out with my coat over my head already sopping wet from the experience I'd just had at the hotel. Standing there in the rain, I dialed my wife's phone. Mary Lou answered on the first ring, as she knew about the important meetings that day. "Why are you calling me from this number?", she asked, then quickly added, "Well, how did it go?" Even before she could get that out of her mouth, I said, "So, are you up for a big adventure?"

And she said, "Uh, what, what do you mean, 'up for a big adventure'?"

I quickly went on to tell her about my demise in the last hour as fast as I could while standing there in the pouring rain. I did try and express some excitement as to what had to lay ahead for us. I said it was 'going to be unlimited and full of possibilities'. She did not share in my excitement. Mary Lou burst into tears and I could hear fear coming from her voice clear as day. I said, "Honey, calm down. Babe, everything will be fine. God has a plan. Let's focus on being guided. We'll talk when I get home." And boy did we talk when I got home.

I knew that the next day when I woke up I would no longer be the CEO and that Tony would not be picking me up. Nor would my Starbucks sugar-free, skinny vanilla latte and *USA Today* be waiting for me in the car. A whole new path before me was going to materialize. My old world was now gone. When I went to bed and slept that night it was clear that I would awaken as a new person. I knew that Home Services Berkshire Hathaway thought they had just fired a CEO, which they had done. But what they had really done was birth a pent up entrepreneur.

This book and the chapters that follow will be part story, part how-to and part journey told from my view on the path of an entrepreneur. And not just for the last five years from when I was fired as CEO from a Berkshire Hathaway company, but for the last 25 years that I have been in the real estate business. What flowed through me in all that time was being an entrepreneur contained in someone else's box. I realized my next path would have to be about being an entrepreneur in my own created box, and hopefully with no limits this time.

Golden Nuggets

 We have limited control over external factors once

they happen.

 We have a great deal of control over our response to

external factors when they do.

 Believe everything happens for a reason. Your job is

to discover why.

 Know all roads eventually lead to an end and new

beginnings.

Chapter **3**
Birth of an Entrepreneur

Before being fired by the corporation that acquired the company I started with originally, I watched an entrepreneurial company become a corporate company. I learned the pros and cons of both models, and how both models affected me and others personally and professionally.

Many people reading this book have either been fired from a job, or they may know someone who has been fired. It may have been as a teenager or an adult, maybe once, or maybe numerous times. Just that word *fired* has intensity around it. The word surely has an ending. On his show *The Apprentice* Donald Trump uses "You're fired!" for dramatic effect. It has a strong ring of finality about it. People get the message in no uncertain terms.

I believe what some people feel is shock. But I think most people, when they're fired, know that something is coming. If you're going to get fired, there's usually an aspect of the relationship with the company and the employer that feels off somehow. You know something is not quite right or in harmony. The disharmony may be around profits, production, or relationships. If you're paying attention, when you look back you will realize you've had a lot of signals along the way. In hindsight I did, too.

Personal Landscape Changes

The emotions about getting fired are pretty close to the same in many people. There is a sense of shock, fear, betrayal of the company to the employee or the person. There is a mix of feelings: anxiety, excitement, shame, relief, panic, possibility, fear, and lots of questions. I think you quickly must dig deeper beyond the shock and imagine how your new path could look. There is also the concern about appearance. How will you look to your peers, your family, your wife or husband, your children, and your friends? Processing all of these things all at once is intense to say the least.

It's just the connotation of being fired, like when someone says the *C word*. People are often afraid to say they have cancer because it's the C word. It brings so much depth and baggage around the concept that it's hard to even bring up the word with people you may want support from. To bring it up is to require others to deal with something they may have their own fears around. In your own vulnerability you have to decide whether you are prepared to manage not only your response to your situation at hand, but in addition to that, the burden your needs may inadvertently bring upon someone else. You may end up supporting them as well as yourself in the process, because it's not an easy topic to look at objectively or rationally. Cancer is much more intense and serious of course than getting fired, but the initial shock and processing can be equally devastating.

When confronted with the word *fired,* people don't know if they should comment or not. They don't know if they should not ask what happened, or if they should get the gory details. They sometimes gloss over it, or dig way too much.

Sometimes people don't call or write, and they might just disappear.

The word *fired* also is one of those electrically-charged topics. It creates a massive amount of gossip inside and outside of companies, adding speculation as to whether people knew/didn't know it was going to happen. People always have an opinion of fair-not-fair, will be missed and 'good riddance' among others.

When I was fired, in hindsight I knew for sure something was coming, because unfortunately in the previous years, I had to fire many of my own people. I used the word *fired* many times for many people. Some of them were personal friends of mine that I'd worked with for years. That is never an easy conversation to digest or to deliver.

The feelings that I had around my own experience of being fired were not near to what I would have expected. I had more of a sense of excitement and completion than I had of fear, anxiety and betrayal. Yes, I definitely felt betrayed, but I immediately popped into a sense of excitement because I had played it out in my mind, that if this happened, what I would do and how I would react to it. I had a remembered sense of confidence and faith it would all work out. It always had and always would. So I knew that my reaction was guided by a higher purpose or a Higher Power. This was going to be one more experience of spiritual trust, as I've always led my life. I knew there were many past obstacles and challenges that had led me to bigger and better things before. I was sure it would again.

What was stunning, however, came in the fashion of how people reacted to me and dealt with me in the weeks and months following my exit from the company. I made a mental note of all the friends and associates that I had and who I expected I could still count on. On one side I listed people I thought would be supportive no matter what. If I didn't have the job title, the boats, the house or the big salary for whatever period of time, who would still support me? I then made a list on the other side of who I was sure wouldn't support me if I didn't have all those things.

The interesting fact I learned along the way was that I was half wrong on 50% of the list both ways. Half of those I thought for sure would be there no matter what had all drifted off and stopped returning phone calls in the following days and months. The support they promised they'd always give me ceased and went away.

On the other list of people that I did not think would support me, I found I was wrong on half of that list, too. People that I had no idea felt strongly showed up to support me, and stayed friends with me afterwards. I maintain a continuing friendship with many to this day.

Wake Up Call

I had an opportunity to talk to one of my friends about this. I asked him the question about why he stayed and supported me. I didn't have the title and boats and all of the "things." His comment was, "Steve, I didn't want to be one of those people who was sucking up to you and trying to take advantage of your position and things."

He stated that he really liked me as a person. He admired who I was, and he was friends with me not because of my stuff and the title I had but because of me alone. That was a real eye-opener for me and really gave me clarity. I could see more clearly how I perceived, judged and expected support from others, and how I supported and expected to support and serve others. This experience was a wakeup call for me in many ways.

A wakeup call usually brings light to more than just the immediate situation. I use the analogy of a pebble in a pond where it radiates out. When you throw a pebble in the pond, it radiates out with waves until it trickles into small waves. It trickles out in concentric circles for quite some time. When you have a traumatic experience like being fired, at first your head is ringing, and your life is ringing. Your decisions are ringing and changing and radiating out, affecting all areas of your life. It all radiates out for quite some time, and then life is never the same. But eventually it calms and the water is still again. I have found that such dramatic changes can often times bring positive things, and positive change. God usually knows what he's doing when he throws that pebble.

With that attitude on my part, what started out as a potential trauma somehow transitioned into opportunity for me, and excitement for a new future. During the fifteen years I was at Prudential California Realty we operated with an entrepreneurial style in the first half of that journey. This suited me very well, and I was able to be instrumental in Prudential's steady growth.

The Entrepreneurial Mind

How could I deal with the intensity of becoming fired with unusual grace, and embrace a forced transition in such an amazing way? Here is an example of a day in my life. You'll see as you read the following, how I have lived my life for many years. The attitudes you notice, my point of view, how I fill my mind with positive, inspiring thoughts, and how I discipline my mind and body, all prepare me to be able to accept and work with what life presents to me.

On this particular day I am sitting in Rosarito, Mexico after a great long Memorial Day weekend with my family. I brought my wife Mary Lou and our immediate family to Mexico. We rented a house on the beach in Los Gavios, which is a great and magical place. It is a lovely little community tucked away in Rosarito where people spend time and live. They surf, they have pools, and they are surrounded by beautiful nature. But it is amazing when you drive into Mexico from the U.S. and see the diversity. On the one hand there is poverty, filth and dirt all around you, but also on the other flip of the coin, magic, beauty and joy equally abound.

The drive down the coastline from San Diego to Rosarito has cliffs, big boulders and the rolling hills embrace the backdrop of the ocean and set the tone. We always play Jimmy Buffett and James Taylor's songs about Mexico to heighten the mood. We just get into the vibe here. When we come into Mexico it changes our vibration and we feel a sense of more peace and a different, slower vibration.

One of the things that I am doing each day since I have been here is making sure I am digging even further into my daily ritual, which consists of doing my daily meditation, my affirmations, my energizing exercises, and my confirmation of my day's intentions. As I sit in peaceful meditation I allow equal time for exploring the darker, needy energies of my mind and soul, as well as swimming deeply in the light. I know that my task in this process is to combine the power of those two energies into one force that then is focused on my definite combined purpose, and intentions for that day. I then focus on my mindset and inner voice (or voices) being aligned in rhythm for one purpose. I understand that time is a commodity and it is one of the most precious things that we have. I strive to be present and in balance always, in each situation, each day and in both energies.

As I sit here again in Mexico contemplating these thoughts, my definite life purpose and my path, I am sitting here looking out over the ocean after completing my walk. I did my guided meditation stored on my iPhone this morning, which is one of my favorite guided meditations, which I've done for years. I have listened to my audio affirmations recorded in my own voice. I listened to them as I ran and did my workout. I sat in the silence and allowed God to radiate through my thought and change my vibration into an even more positive tone for this day.

I sit now and look over the cliff at the great green hills rolling down with cobblestone paths. There are ice plants with trickled flowers of yellows, purples, blues and different textures in between the rolling hills. I look at the palm trees butted up out of the sidewalks and at the bottom of people's patios of the different homes that have their sun umbrellas up and their towels hanging outside their doors. Their surfboards are on their patios and their dogs are being walked up and down paths. I look out into the ocean. Today is an overcast day. It is what people would call a dark day. Instead of being in the darkness and not coming out because there is no sun, I made it a point to come out and enjoy the beauty in this day. There is mist, there are clouds, there is fog, but there is also an amazing massive green ocean, which doesn't look blue today. It does look green. I see about 15 surfers out there. I have seen as many as 30 since I have been here this week.

From this vantage point of peacefulness, I think about my path. I think about my many challenges, opportunities and resources, and I relish in the quality of my many advisors and mentors. I think about my family and the life I want to lead with them. I have a flash of thoughts reflecting back on being fired. I knew I was one of their instrumental leaders building up a company I cared about, and then being a good soldier dismantling it. That hurt. A lot. But my life is not over. My career is not over. In fact, it feels as though it's only beginning. This is just as I've always viewed life, old to new, challenges to opportunity and knowing everything has its season and every tide comes in and goes out, as does the ebb and flow of life. I'm finding ways to turn 'Lead into Gold.'

Creating My Own Piece of the Rock

After I was fired and a forced transition was upon me I made the instant decision to birth a new entrepreneur and start my own new brokerage. I knew instinctively the Universe was moving forward in my favor. I had the attitude 'what if everything goes right?!' I kept that mindset every day, that in every situation the Universe was conspiring to my favor and all was going to go right. Much of the time it did and things just flowed. During this time unexpected partnerships and new business relationships were formed. Past associates and vendors came out in droves to help me and be of service during a time I needed it most. It really felt like magic was being created right before my eyes as I watched every new milestone that was being manifested as we created our new path.

I was in awe and so humbled the many people who called and wanted to offer support. Many stated they wanted to follow and join any new venture I was a part of leading. After exploring numerous opportunities that had strong merit and high possibilities I choose one that seemed like the best right path for me and so many who wanted to join the new march. I looked at big national franchise opportunities, small local partnerships and I considered job offers. I compared all such opportunities to starting a fresh new name brokerage from scratch. I did lots of due diligence in many various ways on all options.

Finally, after two months of deep soul searching and business exploration I decided on the path that hit my gut the best and made the most sense in my analytical mind. Once the deal was consummated and all the details were finalized, the journey had begun. So thus the recruiting marathon began and over a 90-day period we moved over 100 plus real estate agents from Prudential to my new company that I had just partnered with in the market. I was now part of an existing small brokerage and was grateful to have respected local talent and partners to support the new influx of agents and growing team. This turned out to be a great win-win for me and all the agents who chose to follow. A new and clear journey had finally begun.

It all worked perfectly and was a very exciting time for all involved. It is always fun and thrilling to create fresh new things in our lives, especially when you are doing it as a group with a common vision and mission. It is also extra special when you are doing it as the underdog in the story, breaking down all of the barriers and beating all of the odds. You see, in 2009 it was still in the midst of one of the worst real estate markets in recent history, and many felt this could not or would not be done with all the odds stacked against us. But we did do it and we did it in a big way!

Over the first year we gained enough momentum that we had quadrupled the size of the group I had joined, and I had opened four more real estate offices in key and prominent markets in San Diego. We were now a total of eight locations. By two years later we hit 1 billion in gross sales volume of home sales for our company and we created a spot to be the 5th largest real estate company in San Diego. Part of our unique and progressive offering was that we were not just a traditional real estate brokerage, but we had created a real estate Lifestyle services company. I always explained this by asking people to think of Angie's List meets Amazon meets real estate agent and progressive brokerage. We created a concierge of many services to help the clients, ranging from getting their mortgages, getting all the settlement services in line to close their transaction smoothly, and then to help them with all home repairs and needed purchases. We were able to help them with services from flooring, landscaping, appliances and electronics, to pool services, remodels and furnishings. Our goal was to be able to create a one stop shopping experience at good prices with great service long after their transactions had closed. We wanted to create lifetime clients and not just one time deals where we moved on to the next after the deal closed. Exceeding expectations was our mission, and offering new and ongoing services to benefit their lifestyles was our goal.

My team broke all kinds of records during this time. We served many individuals and families over a five-year period, and we had lots of fun along the way. We were also focused on high impact valuable community service. Out of every transaction we closed the agents donated a small portion of their commissions to our company's charitable foundation, and the company matched funds along the way. We did many good deeds with our agents in the community by supporting national and local charities of all types, from the cancer society to the local children's hospital and many more. One of the most rewarding and coolest things we did every year was a local community service day. Think of a local farmer's market or street fair geared fully to various charitable organizations.

We would use a large grocery store parking lot and set up our own little charity camp for the day. We had two or three blood mobiles in the lot, an Astro jump for the kids, food vendors, a table or booth for the cancer association, Children's Rady Hospital, finger painting for the kids, shredding paper services for the community, local animal shelters and adoption services. We had cute dogs and pets there to adopt so some local family could take home a new family member. In the midst of all of this we had an assembly line of packing rice, soy, grains and spices in bags that could be made for a complete family meal. We would send this internationally to places like Haiti and Mexico and keep some here locally. At our height of this endeavor we were packing over 25,000 meals in a single day. To say this was one of the highlights of our time together while building and growing our businesses is an understatement. We all really felt we were making a difference, and making an important impact in the communities in which we lived as well as the global world!

But all of this combined over our five years together did not prevent more unforeseen times of change, transition, transformation and ultimately a new unexpected evolution for all involved. Life is funny with full circles and crossed paths old and new in our lives. I had some very exciting, rewarding and magical times during this five year run after leaving corporate America as an executive. I learned as much in 5 years of being a business owner and CEO of my own company as I did in the 10 years, prior in my life previous. All experiences were extremely valuable and life changing in so many ways, but there is something about being an entrepreneur in the trenches every day that makes a deep impression and understanding from the core that one cannot fully know until they experience this profound and personal journey. There is much joy, pain, collaboration, creativity, frustration and fulfillment that you experience on this path. I highly recommend it but it is not for the faint of heart.

Ultimately this five-year journey included many accolades, challenges and downfalls, two brand name changes, partnerships with other viable and profitable businesses, people who came and joined the journey and those who left, betrayals and some backstabbing, great people and generous gifts and more life lessons. All of that and the details about it are too long and deep to go into here in these writings. That is the beauty of writing and telling your stories to reflect, hopefully to help and inspire others and there is always another day and another story to be told. That is a way of saying this will have to wait until there are future books, articles and videos to unveil these very compelling and telling stories that have helped shape me and others into the people we are now. There have been so many cool and exciting stories that have been birthed and launched from this initial seemingly tragic story of mine. Also intertwined with so many others getting fired in a downsizing economy and world, and how they manifested exciting new lives. But actually in hindsight it just turned out to be another magical example of turning challenges into opportunities, dreams into reality and 'Lead into Gold'!

Doing Well by Doing Good

At the chosen end and completion, at least this time, of the 5-year real estate entrepreneurial journey, I decided to once again reinvent and start a path anew. I had been yearning for many years to branch out into a wider scope and depth of business pursuits. I had desired to start a consulting, coaching, speaking, workshop business while writing books and articles to inspire, help and guide others. I also had aspirations to become a serial entrepreneur getting involved in various and diverse businesses but all in some unique way complementing each other. This was not unlike my previous "lifestyle services" company. Thus the transition began and I finished up my roles and commitments within my real estate firm and charted out new paths and horizons.

As I started my newest business venture, Alchemy Advisors, I knew I had to focus on my ideal client, my ideal market, and who I could serve best. I originally thought I wanted to focus more on market disrupters, crazy out-of-the box entrepreneurs, small start-up entrepreneurs, and mid-size entrepreneurs who are looking to grow larger, or maybe looking to grow and sell. My real interest, where I have the most enthusiasm, is with entrepreneurs. While I was working with one of my coaches, as I've done for twenty-five years, this particular coach suggested that I not cut myself short. He drew a box with corporate on the top, entrepreneurs at the bottom and in the middle he had a big circle and arrows that went from both boxes to the circle.

He said, "What do both of these people have in common?" I said, "Number I probably profit." They probably both want to make a profit and they probably both want to make a difference. So the common denominator is revenue and profits. My bias was that I believed an entrepreneur had more value they were offering to the consumer, and they wanted to make a bigger difference than the corporate world. From my perspective and experience, corporations were just all about profits. My coach reminded me that there are many corporations and companies right now, that yes, they are making massive profits, but they are also doing lots of good in the world.

There is a shoe company called Toms that, every time you buy a pair of shoes, they take another pair of shoes and ship it to a Third World country. They have just exploded over previous years from where they started, and are now a multi-million-dollar organization, while at the same time doing really great work. That is part of their business model.

Zappos is doing a lot with social awareness, employee improvement and cultivating a positive workplace. Starbucks is doing a lot good of things within various communities. Bill Gates, separately from being a CEO, stepped out and is donating much of his wealth to bettering the world in the areas of environment, clean water, healthcare and medical research. Many of these corporations that started out with a few individuals became large and successful. They are on a mission, either from the beginning or now that they are wealthy, to be able to do good.

GE says their employees combined tracked over 1 million hours a year in charitable and community work. Now that's is a lot of good work!

Verizon matches donations for many of the employee gifts to local charities. There are criteria they must meet, but what a great incentive to get their employees involved and rewarded to help others.

LinkedIn has one Friday a month the employees do community collective work as well as more training about giving locally and globally.

As I look at my own brand and value proposition, I focus on like-minded entrepreneurs and corporations who want to make a profit and do good to make a better world. If I know those are my two target market audiences, it will make it easier for me to identify potential clients, versus saying, I can work with corporate or I can work with entrepreneurs. I can do both.

I was concerned that one of my messages was going to be anti-corporate in order to be able to attract the entrepreneurial clients. I knew that a lot of people are entrepreneurs because they are very anti-corporate or they didn't have success, or a satisfying experience, in corporate. Some of them were pushed out of corporate or they were burned out on corporate America, or were not fulfilled. So I was thinking, how am I going to bridge that gap and messaging?

My coach gave me some clarity on that, which was very helpful. When we looked at what I am about personally, or what my company could be about, it is about transition, transformation and evolving to higher places and higher good. This is what I have done in my life from the very beginning. That is why I came up with the name of my consulting company, Alchemy Advisors. Alchemy includes the parables and the legend of The Alchemist transforming lead into gold. It is the chemistry of things and is in combination with minerals, stone and an elixir. It has a mystical, mysterious tone to it. Alchemy also has spiritual references and is focused on transforming and creating with the formulas they are entrusted with to work. In addition, I was also very drawn to the Alchemy name because of the book *The Alchemist* by Paulo Coelho as discussed in prior chapters.

My coach helped me drill that down to adding one more word. I already had transition and transform, but we then came to the next word, which was evolve. So I have come to Alchemy Advisors – Transition, Transform and Evolve. My positioning statement is: "I work with businesses to transform and evolve to higher profits, and do even more good in the world. That is what I do. I help companies to make a difference and to make more profits."

The Three P's

I am on this mission of and theme of "Transition, Transform and Evolve," and the process I created called the three P's. I help people drive Profit, Productivity and Purpose. The three P's of what I do within my consulting and coaching business is that I help people in their companies become more productive, create more profits and have deeper meaning and purpose within their companies, their lives and their communities.

How do I do that? First, through the people there, I start with one person or many within the organization depending, and I dig deep. My intention is to discover their purpose and vision through 360-degree interviews, questionnaires, conducting assessments from the CEO and leaders at all levels, then down through the company. I start from the top, go down to the bottom, then from the bottom to the top. If it is a solo entrepreneur we may do that with family, friends, vendors, or trusted clients, and we redirect our focus and approach as needed.

Next, I want to look into what the average employee or salesperson is producing right now. There are employees on the advertising and marketing side, the administrative side and the operation side, but what is their output right now? What is their workflow? What is their product results? How many people are in the company? How many hours do they work in a week? What do they focus on during that time? What are the goals and objectives for that division or that particular person within the company? How can I help them through my systems, processes, coaching, training, motivation, time management, and communication skills? How can I help employees or salespeople be more productive? My goal is a focus on happiness so they are feeling of value, making a bigger contribution, and are adding more within the organization.

From there people find purpose as they understand how they add to the ultimate goal of helping and improving their company's profits. I help people become more productive. We go from purpose, vision, mission and productivity, and then again back to profits. I think of a pyramid triangle where the bottom of the triangle is transition, in the middle of the triangle is transformation, and then at the top in the little diamond is evolution. So they can see that by doing these certain things with productivity, profit and purpose, I help people transition, transform and evolve. I really like this, and it ties in well with my thoughts about creating value propositions within a brand and for individuals.

I also talked with my coach about was how I can help people overcome setbacks and create new opportunities, thereby helping turn their 'Lead into Gold.' Lead is very heavy. Lead holds things down. You have heard the phrases "That's a lead weight," "You've got a lead weight around your neck," "Throw them in the water and put some lead around them," or "They've got some lead in their shoes." Lead describes something that holds you down, whereas gold is something that is moldable, has value, and shines.

LEAD TO GOLD FORMULA

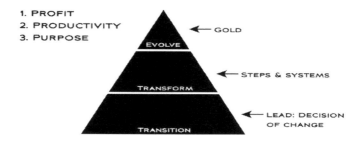

The illustration here shows the realization of desired change in any area of your life. You first must realize you have something you want to transition from and into. Whether it be personal or business, it all starts from the same core base, a 'realization.' Once you have that, then you can determine what you want to transform into.

This process of making the sheer mental effort and then taking the physical steps and actions to transform is one of the hardest in the entire process.

It goes back to what we all know of the concept of Newton's Law of Motion: "What is at rest tends to stay at rest, and what is in motion tends to stay in motion unless acted upon by an outside source." Sir Isaac Newton developed his laws of motion to describe the relationship between a body and the forces acting upon it, and its motion in response to those forces.

The first law says that, when viewed in an inertial reference frame, an object either remains at rest or continues to move at a constant velocity, unless acted upon by an external force.

The second law says the vector sum of the external forces F on an object is equal to the mass m of that object multiplied by the acceleration vector a of the object: $F = ma$.

And the third law states that when one body exerts a force on a second body, the second body simultaneously exerts a force equal in magnitude and opposite in direction on the first body.

But man, oh man, getting things in motion takes a herculean event and energy. You must condition the mind and the body as one. But after you set the intention as to gain success, make the plan. Map the steps into manageable chunks and take your very first step towards that, and then magic starts to happen. For me this outside force is my spiritual connection to God and my innate desire to improve and endure. The Universe 'conspires towards your success.'

It is amazing how you will suddenly summon the Universe and all its many forces and people to help you on your new path. You may get an unexpected phone call from someone who helps fuel your idea. Maybe you run into someone at a coffee shop who has the very thing you need for part of your new idea puzzle. Maybe an unexpected check arrives in the mail from a past refund you forgot about. Maybe a building you needed, that you never imagined would be available, comes up for lease.

The examples are limitless, but you get the idea. Once you begin your transition from your old path to your desired path to transform anew, you will be amazed at how the forces and feelings shift to your advantage. As you transform and grow in the process you will at some point get into 'flow.' We have all experienced flow at some point of our lives. Think about when your day just flows by as smooth as silk. All of your appointments seem to start and end on time, your favorite songs just seem to pop on the radio, you get green light after green light. You have an ease in your step and you feel your energy and thinking is at ease and with an overriding sense of peace and trust that all will be well. This is flow.

During the transition and transform process you will come to some point through your hard work, actions, successes and momentum, and realize you have come to a place that feels heightened for you in consciousness and ease. It starts to feel like this new thing is just becoming part of your DNA and psyche. This is one of the key factors when you know you have evolved. Now you determine the time frame in which you stay at this level and plateau, or if you decide at some point to continue the depth of evolution once again. Only you will know. And the process can be endless.

There may also be times where you feel like you need to step it up a bit even from where you are now. You may also feel you need to take it a deeper level or tweak things just a bit to get it "just right." That is ok to and truly part of the journey. This is all an ongoing process not an event! You may need to take a step back and reassess while you take a look at your progress and how you feel mentally, emotionally, physically and spiritually about your own current transformations. I call this **MEPS-SA** this translates to a Mental, Emotional, Physical, and Spiritual State Assessment.

How is your **MEPS-SA** status at this point in your life?

Once you are at this reassessment state you will find you may need to Redefine and Recommit in a slightly new way to get the new results you desire. I call this being aware when

94

you need to pull in the R-3 Formula. Stop take a deep breath, do a little internal and external analysis with the MEPS reflection and the R-3 reset. You will find this works really well as you continue on your own path of constant transformation and evolving to your desired outcomes.

THE R3 FORMULA

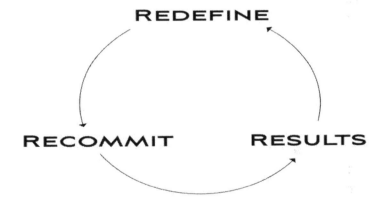

REDEFINE

RECOMMIT   RESULTS

That is the whole point, really. To live life and be in this human experience is an ever changing process. I do believe we are spiritual beings having a human experience, as Dr. Wayne Dyer used to explain so very well. He did such great work in this area and helped shape my life in so many ways. He will be missed, but luckily his wonderful work lives on.

Our innate inner calling that comes from our soul is a universal need to grow and evolve. It is in all of us. My belief is we must feed it or it ultimately leads to unhappiness, discontentment and at the core level a hole in our soul, as I have heard it said.

My greatest desire for this book is for it to be one small reminder to us all to find where else and what else we can transition and transform in our life, ultimately getting to our own individual highest good and purpose. That is the ultimate best gift you could ever bestow on yourself.

Sometimes a Step Backward

After I left Berkshire Hathaway, for about three years everything was flowing wonderfully and the new real estate company I had started was growing leaps and bounds. Yet, the last two years of running my company, I felt something had changed and as though I was starting to be held back. Something seemed to have shifted and changed. I started feeling blocked and my path seemed to be unexpectedly filled with obstacles and challenges. Whether it was with the market, the franchise I had bought and joined, new pending legal issues or my unexpected partner hurdles, I just couldn't seem to make headway, no matter how tenaciously I was trying to stay on top of things.

As I look back, I realize part of the reason for this may have been my ambivalence about my next step. On one hand I was courted by traditional companies to buy my company, create a new partnership and keep me on to lead the organization. These offers were attractive because they not only offered me a way to continue building in the market I knew so well, but a position with an established company meant a certain, regular income and some long-term guaranteed security.

On the other hand, another vision was calling to me of creating a start-up or trying to become a market disruptor. My entrepreneurial mind was bouncing all over the vast possibilities of this path, full as it was of uncertainty and instability.

My goal was to take my intellectual capital and use it while becoming more consciously aware of the skills that I had. I wanted to find ways to break into higher levels of consulting, coaching or business development. Through those avenues I planned to find a way to get to that higher place versus being at just a small entrepreneurial level. I needed to figure that out in my own transition.

In the Drift or On a Path

But in challenging myself this way, there was a sense of being in the drift. I've noticed when I'm in the drift I start challenging myself, and my doubt and fears begin to talk to me. I feel more in a dark, warrior space when I'm in the drift because something triggers me and I get off track. My mind starts playing like a crazy monkey. The drunken monkey cycle starts going. I stop being on track for a day, which leads to a couple of days. I question myself. I get into my self-doubts, self-loathing and self-fear. This is not my usual state of mind, but in this circumstance it can become my constant companion. We are all susceptible to this when we're not on purpose, not on focus, and not clearly doing our mission. We're not in a ritual or pattern. We are not living with an established habit that keeps us on track.

Usually I'm on purpose and creating productive, positive things in my life that lead to successful results. The drift can also at times cause unexpected transition, which can sometimes be negative. A transition is not always positive by any means. Being in the drift can lead to a transition of challenged relationships, jobs, getting fired, losing financial awareness, and losing money because we're not aware of being either focused or unfocused.

I've found the key is to get out of the drift as quickly as possible and get back on purpose, back on habit, on task in order to stay focused on what I'm trying to accomplish in my life. That helps me stay out of the drift.

During this period of drift, I'd been a bit sidetracked when considering market disruptor models as a side path for me while I'd worked in my consulting company. I had to realize that I can't be all things to all people. I had to keep my focus on a path, and I had to stay on that path.

But I do find value in allowing some amount of drift when I'm in a reinvention or transition mode. There is value in taking time to explore and actually look at change, transition, transformation, and moving forward. It's a rich time to be open to and explore all possibilities, opportunities and thoughts. To avoid the downside of the drift, I've learned to do a quick assessment by taking a gut inventory of how I feel about each opportunity. I look at the pros and cons of what it does for my higher purpose, my skills, my involvement, my financial opportunity, and long- and short-term growth. If it's a fit, great! Then I look at pursuing it more deeply. If it's not a fit, I quickly get it off my list so I can keep my mind clear as I explore the next conversation and opportunity, or simply get on with the path I ultimately choose.

We may not find change appealing, but when we look objectively we can see that our entire life is about transition. Every single day when we wake up, we are transitioning to a new day. We are always in some ways in a new environment. We are in a new thinking or in a new mixed emotion and mental thought compared with where we were the day before. So transition really is a part of change in our daily lives. We all know that change is a constant in life, and transition is constant as well. I think this is true for all of us, when we are looking at our business, personal, family, spiritual, or financial lives. We are always in some type of transition. Things are getting older, being reborn, dying, changing hue on a relationship, and there is a transition into a new position or a new level of a relationship. Ultimately, transition isn't good or bad. It just is. The alchemy of turning challenges and transition to opportunity is what I call part of necessities in the entrepreneurial mind.

Curiosity vs. Passion

I want to take a moment here and talk about the notion of passion. Many of us have heard it said to "Follow your passion and everything else will fall into place," "Follow your heart and do what you love and it will never feel like work," and "You really have to have passion around something to be truly successful. Your passion fuels your dream." So what happens if you don't actually know what your passion is at this stage of your life? Maybe you have asked that question of yourself hundreds of times and received numerous answers. Maybe it's vague and it comes and goes periodically. You might think you're passionate about photography one month, and the next month you're passionate about starting an Internet online business in the healthcare field. I run into people often who don't know exactly what their passion is and for some reason they have guilt or shame around that. It may be causing a sense of unhappiness or a sense of depression in their life. If you're in this place, try not to make a negative judgment about it. This is actually more common than you think. We're so bombarded in our lives by people such as our parents, friends, teachers, bosses, our partner, and the media, all of whom has their own ideas of what you should do, that sometimes our own inner voice does get clouded, diminished and lost. And maybe you thought you knew what your passion was when you were young and it has faded and diminished as years have gone by.

Do you know what it takes for you to be successful? If you're struggling with how to find your passion and purpose in this world, it may be helpful for you to do some narrowing down. Sometimes simply being curious, and then more curious, leads to great paths that can help you get in touch with more of your passion.

Eight years ago I met Greg Reid at a Christmas party. The next day he introduced me to the Success Equation, which would forever impact how I view success. Greg Reid is an internationally sought-after speaker and best-selling author who was hand-selected by the Napoleon Hill Foundation to carry on the teachings of Napoleon Hill's "Think and Grow Rich." Greg is also the author of "Three Feet from Gold: Turn Your Obstacles in Opportunities (Think and Grow Rich)." Greg shared quite a few stories with me and asked me some of these questions, such as, "Is it possible for success to come down to a few elements that, when put together, produces a predictable result?"

For those of you wondering about the answers, the Success Equation looks like this:

P + T + A2 + F = Success

That means:
Passion + Talent + (Association x Action) + Faith

I'm yet to find a situation in which this Success Equation did not measure up. Think about how it may work in your own situation or life.

P is for passion. Living a purpose-filled life.
T is for talent. For example, those singers on American Idol have passion, but not all of them have talent.
A is for action because you can have all the talent and passion in the world, but if you don't take steps toward your goal, it won't happen.
A is for association. You are a direct reflection of the people you hang around. Find out how you can meet people who will help you reach your goal.
F is for faith. You must develop an unwavering faith in yourself and your ability to achieve your goals.

How to use this powerful formula:

1. Combine your Passion with Talent.
2. Then multiply it by the right Association, which includes successful people,
3. Add in Action, which includes the concrete steps you can take toward your goal.
4. Then add Faith, which is the unwavering belief in yourself.

In order to effectively apply the success formula, I suggest writing the steps down in your journal or on your device where you can easily reference it:

Passion – Write down a list of ten things that you are passionate about. What do you enjoy doing and what are you willing to do for free?

Talent – Write down a list of ten things you are really good at. What are your key skills and strengths?

When looking at passion and talent, involve your family and friends who know you well. Ask them to remove one item that least describes you from each list. Repeat the process until you have one item remaining on each list. You should narrow it down until you have one remaining item on each list. Doing so will reveal the Passion and Talent variables in the equation.

Association – these are the key people who are part of your life. As the saying goes, you are the average of the five people you surround yourself with. Think of the five people you surround yourself with the most. Are they supportive of you? Do you feel you can learn from them? Ask yourself if they are role models for the type of person you want to become.

Action – Ask yourself every day whether or not you are moving in the right direction towards your goals. Re-evaluate your actions, and determine if you need to make adjustments to continue heading on the right path.

Now add Faith to the mix, and start moving towards your goal. I suggest you write your own success equation as you're heading onto your new path. Remember, this is not an overnight formula to success. It takes time to build.

I have found that this process helps me as I continually turn our lead into gold for myself and others, and as I continue on my own journey of transition and transformation to my highest good. I truly believe these types of exercises can help anyone who is focused on improving in life, and seeking greater meaning and purpose for their future.

Keep the Faith and Dig Deeper

Regardless of the reason, if you find yourself in this place first I'd say give yourself a break. Don't beat yourself up. At least acknowledge to yourself that you're honest enough to realize and admit that you have further to explore and uncover before you authentically commit to the big "passion" that may exist for you out there. However, there are a few things I would encourage you to do if you find yourself in a spot. One is to journal. Take time to sit quietly with yourself in a peaceful place that you enjoy. Whether it is the beach, the woods, a lake, a great private hotel room, or a peaceful room in your own house, start writing. Ask yourself some of the following questions:

- What did I love to do as a kid?

- What was I most fascinated about when I was in school?

- What classes were easiest for me? Where did I get my best grades?

- Where did I seem to get the most praise from a family member or friends as I was growing up?

- Who did I consider a mentor or an idol as I was growing up? In my life now?

- When I watch TV or movies what am I most drawn to?

- When I read books or blog articles, what captures my attention and keeps it the longest?

- When I think about different things I've done in my life, where did I have the most excitement or joy?

- When I'm on social media and I'm scanning through the sites, what captures my attention? What increases a sense of jealousy in me when I see someone doing something that looks intriguing to me?

- What did I want to start that I was passionate about that I never followed through on or completed?

- On my days off in my free time what do I most like to do?

- When I travel on vacation what areas or activities am I most drawn to?

- If I'm only given five key words and I could search online to unlock a key that turns 1000 bucks, what words would I choose?

- Where does my heart and soul seem to come most alive when I think about life in general?

As you're writing and journaling, some of these questions can prompt some great answers that lead you down an unexpected path. Maybe it uncovers something you had left buried, and it somehow scratches the surface and brings it back to life. Whatever may happen from this exercise, take it and roll with it and keep journaling. I find that if I journal for a few days and just freely write and let flow whatever comes out of me onto a pad of paper, it sometimes mysteriously unveils things in my subconscious that need to come out. The sheer act of writing things down gets your mind activated. Speaking to your heart starts conspiring to the Universe to create more thought, and potentially actions and deeds.

I also suggest taking time to write down what you're really good at. What do you feel are some of your top strengths and what comes to you easily in work or your daily life? At the same time write down what you don't like to do, whether it be in your job, household or your daily life. Sometimes the sheer act of writing these down can start showing a pattern that may guide you towards certain areas to explore further within your career paths or hobbies. In addition, if you have someone you really trust and respect and whose opinion you value, I would recommend asking them to do some of these exercises on your behalf. It's really powerful if someone can give you a written description as to how they view you and your strengths, challenges, weaknesses, gifts and natural abilities. Make sure this is someone who knows you well and who will be honest, but also kind and loving in their approach.

I would also recommend using Google or YouTube to start searching for things you're curious about that may come from some of these writings. Sometimes putting into keywords will bring up really awesome videos of people doing amazing things in their life related to giving back to the world or following their own passion. It could be you'll find an item that will spark something in you that allows you to explore some new path you never expected before.

Maybe there is not a big 'Ah-ha! I found my passion moment!' And maybe there is, but it may come in small waves. It may build up step-by-step until you realize you've grown into something that you're really passionate about. I advise and counsel people that this is a great place to start asking yourself:

- What am I curious about?

- What would I like to know more about?

- What intrigues me when I listen to others speak?

- Related to the above questions, what sparks curiosity in me?

It is enough to start there and then take the first relevant step to become better educated and learn more about your curiosity topic. There are so many ways to learn in this day and age of the Internet, videos, blogs, books, workshops, adventure travel seminars ... the list goes on and on. Pick a topic or two you want to explore and start scratching at the surface of that and dig deeper. You will probably find there's a reason you are drawn to this particular topic, industry, hobby, art, person, and you may find a sense of bubbling up excitement as you explore it. Just the sheer act of committing to exploring one or two things at a time that you're curious about can lead to a very fulfilling life of purpose, happiness and joy. This active exploration is one of the key factors of our evolution as human and spiritual beings. I believe this is the essence of the 'Lead to gold' philosophy. You can transition from one place of your life to another. You can transform your thinking about your evolution to a higher understanding consciousness. When you get to this new place it may be just the ticket you need to get on the ride of

106

your lifetime. And if for some reason it doesn't transpire it will surely be a great journey, regardless of whether you ever reach a final destination.

The bottom line is even if you don't know what your big driving force and passion might be, you surely must know what you have a little curiosity about. This is enough. Start there. Just as a fire starts with one little spark that can a fuel raging fire, so can a little dose of curiosity eventually fuel the wave of passion that you may ultimately seek.

Make it Part of Your Day

On a daily basis I've been using some kind of a scorecard to track daily the key areas of my life. I picked up this little tip from a men's workshop I attended. This was a very powerful intensive, workshop. Afterwards I worked with the coach and trainer who conducted the workshop, Raul Villacis. It was great reinforcement of lessons learned that helped me deepen and fine-tune my current existing rituals and daily practices. Afterwards I worked with a coach for a few months. The simple key areas I block out with a scorecard are: I. Body, 2. Being, 3. Business, 4. Bonds. These four things can easily be a summary of some of the goals in key areas we have been talking about in this book.

I give myself one point for each of these key areas. If I make significant effort in that day to be aware and make a difference, I get points in the following ways. In my Body I get .5 point if I stay on my vegan healthy eating plan, and I get .5 point if I do my daily regulated exercise for a total of one point. In my Being, which is my spiritual connection, I get .5 point when I do some form of meditation during the day, and .5 point when I do some type of spiritual reading, for a total of one point. In my Bonds I get .5 for expressing and showing love to my family in some obvious way, and .5 for showing love and appreciation to someone else outside my family, for a total of one point. Last, but not least, for my Business I get .5 for working in my business moving things forward and taking key action steps on my daily goals, and .5 for working on my business by doing some kind of planning or creative effort that will help my business for the future. I can achieve four points in one day or total of 28 points for the week.

This is a very simple, easy exercise you can put on your calendar or write on a piece of paper, in your iPhone, or you can create some fancy Excel spreadsheet. There are many customized ways to keep yourself accountable to your goals. I have included a sample worksheet here and a blank one for your own use.

	BODY	BEING	BONDS	BIZ	TOTAL
MONDAY	1	1	1	1	4
TUESDAY	1	.5	1	1	3.5
WEDNESDAY	1	1	.5	1	3.5
THURSDAY	1	.5	1	.5	3
FRIDAY	1	1	1	1	4
SATURDAY	1	1	1	.5	3.5
SUNDAY	1	1	1	.5	3.5
				WEEKLY TOTAL	25

Life Balance Chart. If you would like a blank copy, please visit leadtogoldbook.com/giveaways

The beauty of this is even though it seems like work, having a structure keeps you mindfully focused on the major key areas of your life on a daily basis. By being aware of these things personally, I find I am more present to whatever current situation I'm in. It helps me stay focused, present and artfully engaged in flowing and moving through my day. It may seem a little cumbersome at first having all of these goals and plans and accountability points while trying to be present in the present moment. But I can assure you I know you can handle it. The mind and spirit do amazing things when combined in one focused effort, in the body, and in this our universal surroundings quickly fall into place.

It's very important, once you have written your goals, to put it out into the universe. Have some accountability so you find ways to be in harmony, flow and joy to help you let everything just naturally unfold. You will quickly see and understand the concept that what Paulo Coelho talks about in the Alchemist that "the universe is conspiring toward your success", once your mind is finally made up, and you know your mission and plan is attainable.

There are also significant factors that can keep you present in the present moment if you're wondering how to be even more aware of exercising this desired state of mind. I have learned, just as actors memorize scripts for films and plays, that our minds can memorize key new efforts and habits that can change our thinking and better our lives.

Resistance

The reality of resistance in our lives is a powerful force. I experience resistance on a daily basis. The invisible force of resistance is one of the strongest forces I have encountered during the process of transition to something more, something better, and something higher, whether it be in business or in life. I know as I've been writing this book numerous things have come up in my life, including procrastination, excuses, long gaps of working on any other thing that may only take me away from my intended project. I set times daily, or at least a few times a week to have worked on this book and many, many times I was pulled off course. Business matters, family matters, getting preoccupied in email, social media, web research, shuffling papers or anything else that seem to pull me off track of reaching the goal to write and finally birth this book.

I know that in other areas of my life this invisible field of resistance also has existed. This has been going on since the beginning of time. When I've tried to lose weight, start a new exercise program, get up earlier, eat better foods, save more money, spend less money, watch less TV, start a new hobby, start a new business or just consciously decide to better myself or my life in any way, I encounter resistance. I used to think this was just not having enough willpower or commitment. But I've come to learn and believe that this is a real force and that it exists in all of our lives. Gravity is real and proven all the way back to the days of Aristotle, Galileo, and Newton. Newton's original formula was:

$$\text{Force of gravity} \propto \frac{\text{mass of object 1} \times \text{mass of object 2}}{\text{distance from centers}^2}$$

Just as people finally came to comprehend the power of gravity and the scientific formulas behind it, so I believe the power of resistance will come to be studied even further as time progresses. It is real and powerful, and is connected to our desire to evolve and change, as well as to the force and size of our dreams.

Do you ever notice that sometimes the bigger your dream, the harder it is to get off the ground and the more resistance you can encounter along the way of getting it birthed? This is a power resistance. So on those mornings when you know you want to get out of bed and go to the gym, the force in your mind, in your reasoning and in your excuses seems equal or greater to the original intention you had of working out and getting healthier. The question is which force is going to win out? Do you break through that energy and get your feet on the floor and get on your workout clothes and get busy, or do you roll over, turn off the alarm and fall back to sleep in your warm comfy bed? The outcome of this will tell you who won, resistance or the power and force of your dream breaking through the invisible bonds of resistance.

Just as I have referenced The Alchemist at the beginning of this book, I also recommend for anyone who is a writer or is looking to create any new dream to read the book The War of Art. It has been described as nothing less than Sun-Tzu for the soul. In it the author describes the enemy that every one of us must face. The book outlines a battle plan to conquer this internal foe and then points just how to achieve the greatest success. It addresses the naysayer in all of us but focuses on making sure you find ways to not have that be your dominant voice. The War of Art emphasizes the resolve needed to recognize and overcome the obstacles of ambition, and then effectively shows how to reach the highest level of creative discipline. Think of it as tough love for yourself.

Earlier last year I made a commitment after I started my new consulting company Alchemy Advisors, to make myself my number one client. But I knew that advising my number one client about what they can do to get their new dream off the ground would include advice about having the healthiest body, mind and soul they could create. So for me that started with a new commitment of a radical food plan, a daily workout plan, a daily meditation plan, and adding in some new hobbies to keep it fun and fit altogether. I became a vegan, took a radical step to dramatically change my daily eating habits and my relationship with food. This was supported and guided by a health coach who had 40 years in the business, who was a previous surgeon and medical doctor. He now does amazing work in the holistic preventative healthcare industry.

I hired a trainer to come to my house three days a week to eliminate excuses and to have another warrior to help me break through the power of resistance. I beefed up my commitment to daily meditation beyond what I've been doing for years. I went to a Kung Fu studio and joined as a new student. I challenged myself to do something I've been saying for years I wanted to do in the field of martial arts. All of these things combined helped me to have a collaborative effort and create great momentum to break through massive resistance as I started this process. There were many challenges, trials and tribulations along the way. But once I got the momentum and once I got things moving forward I'm gratefully down almost 60 pounds from where I started. I continue to be a vegan and follow this complete program to this day. I never went off my plan of eating vegan foods even once during this entire process, and I still eat as a vegan today.

Once my mind was made up and I committed, I got all of the support systems in place I could possibly muster. I jumped in and started down the path. Believe me there were days and situations where I was challenged and could almost physically see the cloud of resistance coming in, looming around me. It was almost like a cloud at the top of the mountain as you look out on a horizon in one of those amazing nature pictures. I could see it trying to seep into my mind, soul, psyche and my body. I had to fight it off by having systems and tools in place that allowed me to not succumb. I wanted the breakthrough to what I knew was on the other side. What I knew was on the other side of the resistance and the fear that surrounds all of these decisions we make is great power. The sheer act of breaking through becomes the empowerment we need to tap into the energy, and into the reservoir of power in the experience itself.

Just as I can't physically see gravity, I know resistance exists and I don't debate it. In my life when I'm trying to turn something from 'Lead to gold' in any area, I calculate into the formula of my approach the reality that resistance is one of the key ingredients I need to factor in. Just as we talked about creating business plans and life plans, you also have to create a plan for your success in your desire to transition and transform. Not only does it include the steps in your goals and business plan, but it includes the things you can put into place to battle and combat the reality of resistance when it comes in to sabotage you and steal your dream. The key factors are knowing what your base foundation is and why you desire change in the first place. It's being aware of how committed you are to making this change and what will be the end result as you evolve to this new place in your life. Focus on that outcome and how you will feel, look, who you will help, and what will you achieve. Having a coach, mentor, support group, daily written re-commitments, your journal, audio goals, dream boards, social media forums and so much more will aid in your success. These items can be some of the factors that help you have just that little extra push to not succumb to the resistance and go backwards.

In addition, preplanning to have your weapons and tools in place when resistance shows its ugly face will be one of the keys to your success. Many times as I've traveled on business out of town and to seminars, workshops and business meetings. I've had to protect my desire for being a vegan at the highest level. I pre-planned and brought food with me. I carried a cooler to my hotel room. I requested special food needs before I got to events from the event planners. When going to family events or parties I would make sure I ate prior to or brought my own food with me. I had to plan ahead as I knew resistance was always looming and ready to sabotage my new path to my new horizon. These are just a few examples of some of the things you can do related to eating and food.

Expand this thinking related to other things you may be doing your own life. Maybe you're looking for promotional work, or maybe you want to learn a new language. You may want to go back to college, or maybe you're seeking a new relationship. Whatever it might be, know that resistance will surround part of this decision-making process. Resistance will be ever present looming like a backseat driver waiting to chime in any moment. Think about what you can do in your own situation to set yourself up for the biggest success possible. Reduce the possibility for temptation and giving in to this negative dark force trying to hold you back. You have to want the dream, the desire and the change more than you want to stay where you are. The problem is that resistance wants you to stay exactly where you are. It is not unlike the story you've probably heard about lobsters trying to crawl out of a boiling pan of water while the other lobsters keep trying to pull the one getting to the top back in. Maybe this is similar to that phrase 'misery loves company.'

The good news is even if resistance wins in a situation here and there, or on a day here and there, you can always get back on track. You can recommit, refocus, and you can pick yourself back up and move forward. Use the R-3 formula. You can learn what didn't work in that situation and prep and plan for what you're going to do differently next time you're in battle with resistance. In writing this book I just kept moving forward, knowing that I wanted to get it completed and to get my messages out to the world. I knew that I hoped and planned that even if one person could be helped by my messaging, it would be worth the efforts that I was putting forth during this time of writing a book. Resistance did win many times, but since you're reading this book you clearly know who the victor was at the end of the day. My motto now as I look in the face of resistance is "Bring it on!" Bring on the best you've got because now that I know how real you are, and that you exist, and that you will be my unwanted companion throughout my lifetime, I now know how to work within my own formulas to create the best Alchemy and the 'Lead to gold' process more easily and smoothly in my missions and goals moving ahead.

Golden Phrases

When you think of phrases around gold you may remember things like, "they have a heart of gold," "that is good as gold," "everything they touch turns to gold," they have a gold mine on their hands." Thus it has come to pass that having something of more or higher value can be the gold consciousness versus being weighted down in lead thinking or mindset.

Our currency within the world has been founded on precious metals. Gold has always been one of the most precious metals. To this day gold still holds its value, and it normally increases in value because it is a commodity. There is only so much of it. It can be shaped, molded, turned into bricks, jewelry or coin, and it can be reshaped. I love that lead is heavy and gold is glittery, but it has value, and has the capability to transform. Gold also represents love and commitment in marriage. A ring around your finger symbolizes union and choice. It also represents love because when you are giving or wearing jewelry, it is a symbol of emotion and feeling. Changing our focus and thinking to create the words, actions and deeds that can manifest more of our values in our lives is key. This is where vision, goal setting, planning, action and accountability become the ingredients in the formula needed to manifest your own golden results.

Part of my slogan for employees and salespeople is, "I can help turn 'Lead into Gold' by helping employees find more purpose, passion and productivity."

These steps alone will help shift thinking and fuel transition and transformation. This process can help companies turn willing, but unproductive, sales people into more productive sales people. If there are pricing issues and lack of perceived value of their product, coaching or sales calls, research and transition can turn it into more value and gold. I often hear people say they love their job or work. This is usually because they have some passion around it. It also makes them feel of purpose and value. All human beings want to be heard and valued.

My coach and I recently discussed selling from where you are. I still have a coach to this day that helps me stay accountable and focused on my life and business goals. My new coach has a unique blend of understanding online marketing in an expert way, yet he also has a deep spiritual base that works really well for me. As you're looking for coaches and mentors in your life always seek out people who have common beliefs as you do but skills, knowledge and wisdom that you still seek.

Anytime I am coaching or consulting with someone, where are they? Where is their mindset, their skill base? Where is their thinking? Where is their thermostat set for their own positions in life, and where are they comfortable? I have been at high-stakes tables with high-end success players like Warren Buffett and the people surrounding him. I am comfortable sitting at a boardroom table with other executives while brainstorming, guiding and leading. I am also comfortable buying and living in a multi-million-dollar home, because I have lived in one. That is where I am selling from.

But it was not always that way. I had to re-set my own internal thermostat and thinking as I evolved. So, sell from where you are or where you are comfortable, even if you are not fully there now. Although my life is different now, there were times in the early days when I had to have roommates to help pay the rent. I had a car repossessed in my early life, and a challenge paying bills. That's where my mindset's thermostat was set. Back then I was constantly asking, "How do I get out of this place, and how do I change it?"
Remember it takes Newton's Law of Motion outside forces and help. So take charge and change it if you need to, and

find ways to reset your own thermostat. Keep this thinking in mind when you are dealing with others. Everyone has their own internal thermostat as to where they feel comfortable. The more you can assess and find out where they are coming from, the easier you will be able to connect and sell from where they are!

Golden Nuggets

 Apparent setbacks can actually become wakeup calls to greater opportunity.

 Finding a place of peace within ourselves, and looking at what we love in our lives, can help set us on a new and better path.

 Get clear about the desired change you would like. Write about your passion, talent, association, action and faith. Explore what you've been curious about in your life.

 Remember to try the Success and the R-3 Formula.

 Notice any resistance and be prepared to support your path to change despite challenges that may appear.

Chapter **4**
How to Materialize the Dream

How do you transition from knowing your higher purpose or having a calling, to putting that into a concise, direct, focused plan of action? How do you create clear measuring points and metrics, timelines and goals, all situated within a particular format that works for you? I'll share with you how I've learned to do this for myself.

It isn't a passive exercise for me. Rising up the ladder to the CEO role was done through conscious focus and effort on my part. I created it. I manifested it. I worked hard. I burned the candle at both ends at certain times. First, I helped others reach their goals. As you help others reach their goals first, your rewards will follow. I created a lot of revenue for the company. I exceeded goals. I was driving revenue by recruiting people and helping real estate salespeople become more productive. I created a lot of good relationships along the way. I continued to help people feel good, and I evolved.

I enhanced my training skills and learning skills, and my own sales skills. I went to executive classes and workshops. I had mentors. I hired coaches. I clearly was mapping myself, creating and manifesting all of the skills and talents needed, to becoming the CEO of Prudential California Realty, a Berkshire Hathaway Home Services company.

You remember me sharing with you the moment I was fired, when I was standing in the rain at the pay phone. I knew in my gut how to follow the right path to take for a new creation at any particular time. This includes the moment I was standing in the rain at a pay phone with my wife in tears. I knew I was going to turn 'Lead into Gold,' and was then turning myself into an entrepreneur. And I do admit to a bit of fear, yes, but mostly excitement, completion, anticipation, and a sense of possibilities and of new paths ahead. I also realized that this was going to take a lot of hard work, a lot of transition and a lot of creation. Newton's Law of Motion was going to serve me well. Luckily I knew something about myself, that I had been capable of manifesting things most of my life. In the early days I didn't understand exactly what all that meant. I just felt my direction and new path, and went after it. As I've grown older and wiser, I've learned the power of creation, the power of manifestation, the power of gestation, and the laws of attraction, as well as the power of consistent hard work. I knew that I was going to have to use all those skills and more.

A Deeper Knowing and Trusting

As I put the receiver back down on that pay phone, dripping wet on my way back to my car, I felt something inside of me, within my gut. With water dripping off my nose I took off my water-drenched suit coat and threw it in the back seat of the car. I sat there contemplating and digesting what this was going to be, and within my gut, instantly, I knew that I was going to go create my own company. And I knew that no matter how difficult or challenging the path ahead would be, that was exactly what I was going to do. I didn't know how it was going to come to pass. I didn't know how I was going to create the large amounts of money it would take to make this happen. I didn't know all of the details, but I knew clear as day that it was going to get created and it was going to happen!

That knowingness, a gnawing at my gut and my soul, had been there for some time. Actually it probably went back to the day that I sat in that CEO chair on my very first day in my new position. I always thought this was going to be it and the final path of my career. And now we know it was not. At the time I expected I would be sitting in that chair for many, many years ahead, and it might even be the apex of my career. But I knew even in that moment as I first sat in that chair, that this was not the final path for me. I knew there was something else coming and calling. So in hindsight, by being fired I was actually freed from my old 15-year path with this company, freed for a new journey. I had many, many highs and lows along the way, as we all do in life, but I had great fondness for what that path had been. Yet my gut and my Higher Power connection knew that something new was going to be created. And now freed, I was out to manifest and create that something new.

People ask me all the time how I felt about this coming to an end after all of those years. They knew how much this path and company had meant to me. Was I sad, was I depressed, was I devastated? These are very valid and normal questions when someone is in this situation. However, what I shared with them was there was actually a sense of completion and peace. It's kind of like if you've been reading a very long book for a very long time. You've picked it up and put it down many times, but you've always stayed with the story. Then there is that day you finally come to the last chapter, to the last page, and you close the book. You're left with the thought, "WOW, I didn't quite think that story was going to end that way. But what a really great book."

So the manifestation probably came from just really constantly tapping into my Higher Power. I don't know what you call your Higher Power or your Higher Source, but for me, I call that God. I simply find that 'God' is the easiest way to sum it up. I have always had a sense of connection into a consciousness, a knowing that there's something greater than myself. There is something much greater than I as a human being can encompass, and I know there's something much greater than us collectively as human beings. All you have to do is look around at nature, look at the sky, look at the universes and how the sun knows to come up every day and the tides know to ebb and flow. I don't think there's any dispute that there is a higher energy, a higher purpose, a higher plan or the science of things that none of us profess to fully understand. So for me, I call that a Higher Power. God is the sum of all that is, in this universe and all universes.

Along my journey of being a man, a salesperson, a manager, a leader, a husband, a father, a grandfather, a friend... all along the way I have known that, as Wayne Dyer so eloquently has put, that I am a spiritual being having a human experience. I've always resonated with that phrase because I have known that to be true. And I knew that my path and my desire to be successful, to achieve status and wealth, was only one of the things that I was put on this planet to do. I knew this because I was tapping into a Higher Source, Higher Power, and higher consciousness. I did this through many sources such as prayer, reading, meditations and affirmations, writing, and attending church or a temple. I knew the only way to success financial, status, purpose or otherwise was to do it by serving and creating value.

For me, those paths brought me into seeking out, reading and understanding about the different paths, philosophies and religions from East to West. I found I really do resonate with the Buddhist-type thinking and principles and the Eastern philosophies, although I was brought up in the west in a very traditional Catholic faith. I've now merged the philosophies in a way that fits for me. What I'm saying here is that I always had a higher purpose and a higher knowing. I remain eternally grateful to my parents who gave to their five boys a base foundation in core religious beliefs. Most of all their example of how they practiced and lived their faith as best they could themselves left a positive impression on me. I choose to explore beyond my base faith. At the core it gets down to love, which is truly the base of all religions and spiritual faiths. I believe that whatever your path, you must always tap into your own higher source to sustain you.

That said, I've known from a very, very young age that if I listened, stopped, sat in silence, followed my gut, if I prayed and waited for answers, they would come. I thought and I knew, "Everything happens for a reason," and then I looked within that particular reason for signs about what I was searching for. I always knew that I would be guided. And so I have been. I have always followed my gut. I have always followed my instinct. I have always followed some unknown nudging, even if I couldn't explain it or understand exactly how it was going to work out. I faithfully followed it.

In addition to being intuitive and following my higher purpose and my higher path, I have also been a planner. I've learned this through mentors, workshops, corporate, personal, and company accountability, and trial and error. I have learned that anything you can think, say, do and put from thought to word, to action, to deed, becomes a reality. That anything that you think about and focus on expands. And I realized if I could get very detailed with that in the planning process, beyond my intuitive, Higher Power consciousness, I knew that would be a very powerful manifestation combination. And it has proven to be so.

This has shown up in my life in various forms. Sometimes it's through people or situations that speak to me as clearly as my own defined thoughts. Sometimes it's like a series of green lights in life, confirming my way, where everything just seems to line up.

Seeds of My Own Company

Sometimes there are seasons in our lives where things aren't lining up so well. It may seem like one red or yellow light after another. This happened to me, culminating on the day I was fired as a CEO of my previous company. I had brought in many talented people that I both learned from and added value to, and I truly cared about this company. I was very humbled knowing that I added as much back into that company as I was able to learn and take. I had a meaningful exchange with the company and the people there in terms of income, knowledge, expertise and being mentored by others. So when I did have those dark days and thought, "Why am I doing this?" and "I don't want to take this hassle from the bosses," in those moments, I would reflect, "What would it be like if I ran my own company? What would it be like if I created my own path?"

I had actually started writing out my ideas a few years prior to this. I created my ideal business plan about what I would like to achieve in a company or my own organization. I'd had that plan sitting on a shelf for years. So I knew in the moment when I was dripping wet sitting in my car, sitting in my own silence, that I was going to implement my plan. That night I pulled out the business real estate company business plan. I looked at what it entailed, polished it up, and fine-tuned it based on what I immediately knew was happening in the marketplace at this particular time. I took the next day off and I got right into the planning process.

My plan covered elements about creating the ideal consumer experience, the process, and service offerings. I reviewed how I planned to deliver it, how the marketing would work, and a description of an ideal team. I wrote about the kind of sales people and team members I needed. I had considered whether I would be the sole owner or if I would have partners. Picking a business partner can be equally as important as picking a marriage partner, and can be the life and death of a company. I described my preferred executive and partnership structure and team, and a schedule of when to bring on how many people in phases. I answered other questions, such as: What will be needed for a team to get this product offering out and in service? When would I need capital and how much? How would I fund and run this business?

Even though this transition forced upon me one big red light that slammed on my brakes temporarily, it was only a few months later that I began to see green lights again. This only happened after exploring numerous opportunities to re-invent myself. But once I made a decision, a final commitment, and took swift action going down that path, I was able to receive one green light after another. This happened in the form of investment capital, great building leases, attracting great management and sales people, and great momentum. Things just started to flow very quickly and smoothly.

Working with the Dream

The creation and manifestation of the dream is a very interesting process to go through. It's very hard to put your head around the exact thing that turns the dream into becoming a reality. It's not as easy as saying two plus two equals four because a lot of things have to happen. For me, the number one thing is to be able to believe it! You have to actually birth the dream inside of you. You then have to articulate your dream, and be bold enough to get it out into the world.

So, what is that thing that calls you inside, that scares you, but excites you enough at the same time? The dream that makes you want to say, "It feels scary. But what's the dream that would really push me beyond where I am right now? That would be so exciting and fun, and it would really make a difference in my life and the lives around me. What makes my heart sing?"

That's probably the best place to start with one of your dreams. A dream can be about an idea, a relationship, having a child, moving to a certain area, taking a boat trip around the world, building a company, starting a new brand, getting a promotion at work, or even learning to surf. Whatever you're inspired to dream about, here are some key elements that can add up to making this a reality for you.

Manifesting Step by Step

The first thing to do in order to manifest and materialize a dream is to articulate your dream. Get crystal clear on what the dream is and write it down. Then from there, figure out the time period you want to be able to materialize this dream. I had goals, dreams and lifetime plans from 90 days, six months, one year, three years, five years, 10 years, and to 20 years. I've found for myself and people in general, that we often over-estimate what can get done in a year. However, people underestimate what they can get done in three years. The more detailed and specific you are with timelines and expectations, the better your plan has a chance of materializing.

When I think about dreams, I don't think about them in just one isolated area. I think about materializing the dream as a quilt, or in a sphere and a globe of my own life that radiates out well beyond an isolated dream. You may not choose to do it that way, as maybe it's too overwhelming. But I like to sit and think about all that's possible. One of the ways I've done this is to take a notepad and just write out different categories. I write about my overall life, and how I want my life to look in general.

Here are the key categories I used to map out the rest of my overall plans:

1. Business career

2. Family and relationships

3. Money and investments

4. Health and fitness

5. Personal and professional development

6. Community and charitable community work

7. Spiritual inner peace

8. Mental goals, things to learn, know, create and become wiser

9. Emotional life, emotional state and dreams to create

10. Contribution to the world

These general categories would be mental, physical, emotional, and spiritual and what I want materially in my life. I know this is a lot of categories to consider, but that's how I did it. I started putting those categories at the top of the page, and then I would just start writing. Sometimes I would sit and write for a couple of hours at a time without taking a break. I usually block out a long weekend. My wife and I do this at the end or the beginning of each year. Normally we make it a long weekend getaway. We go to a lake or to a special place where we know we won't be interrupted. We enjoy part of the day, and then we write the rest of the day and work on our own goals. Picture a hotel room with flip charts taped all over the walls. They're calling to us while we're out at the pool enjoying the sun, waiting for us to return and help manifest them into further reality.

Assuming I have the luxury of dying of old age, I hope to be able to be on my deathbed and have said a proper goodbye to everybody. I want my last words and emotions to feel as though I've lived every ounce of me, that there are no other chapters or pages to turn in a book of my life. If this is true when I'm on my deathbed, then what would I want to be able to say, to explain the life that I had led? What would I want others to have known and felt from knowing me? How can I start creating more of that reality now?

How does that life canvas look? What is the painting of your own life? Think about a painter who has a blank canvas envisioning the most beautiful picture he or she ever painted. They have to first imagine it being painted onto the canvas before they can ever really make their first brush stroke. One of my first dreams was that I would live life healthily, full of energy and free of any major diseases or traumas. That I have the luxury to map out my plans. I have the energy, health, fitness and desire to rally and create. Without health, nothing else works very well. Health is wealth. I make sure I focus big goals there. I have definitely had health issues in my day. I'm sorry to say, I've been on my deathbed more than once. But in the last several years I've been very healthy. I'm currently at the most optimum health I've been in my adult life, by choice.

131

Couple Goals

My wife and I also have our couple goals. Some of them turn out to be similar or the same, and some of them are completely opposite. We make sure that on the important core values of our family, our spirituality, our travels, and the dreams we are creating together, that we share a lot of common goals. We talk about the ones we have in common and the ones that are not. It opens up great dialogue for deepening our relationship on having common goals in all these areas. The result is that we both end up with our own very detailed individual goals, being supported by the other. And we also have our couple goals that we can bring to fruition together throughout the coming year. I highly recommend this.

Plan to Follow Up

Once I have all of my goals written down, I go back to each section and I say, "Okay, let me think about and really consider how I'm going to make a contribution of time, energy and effort." I ask, "Do I really want to do the work and invest the time, energy and effort to achieve 'X'?"

If the answer is yes to these questions I add it to one of the goals section and I make it part of my permanent list. If the answer is no it gets crossed off my list. From the notepad, I turn the goal into affirmation cards. I take out my index cards and I write down "I am..." statements. For example, I may write:

- I am fit, trim and healthy.

- I am at my goal weight of 175 lbs. with a waist size no greater than 34 inches.

- I eat clean, healthy meals daily that are vegetarian and vegan based.

- I exercise with excitement and enthusiasm each and every day.

- I am making a contribution to others by volunteering at least three hours a week in community service.

- I am a best #1 best-selling author on Amazon by the end of 2016.

In this day and age of technology, you can just pull out your mobile phone or iPad and record all this electronically in minutes. There are so many apps and programs to record these electronically. You can email the audio to yourself. You can post it on your private Facebook page. You can record a video of yourself and play it back to yourself later. However, I personally still like the physical act of writing them down. It seems to be more real for me.

I find this very powerful. By materializing the dream and putting it all down on paper, I then read it out loud while sitting in my car with great inspirational music playing in the background. This is like having my own private soundproof recording studio right in my driveway. Next, I read all of my goals and affirmations with great excitement, enthusiasm, at a good pace, so when I listen to it again it really drills down into my mind, emotions, and soul. I break these up into 3, 5, 10, and 20 minute segments so I can use them in various situations. I pick whichever background music or audio length that is appropriate for the situation I'm in, whether running, working out or driving.

We all have voices in our head all day long talking to us. The strong subconscious mind is always at work. Unfortunately, many of those voices have negative, critical, doubtful, shameful, or harsh words that far from inspire us. These get reprogrammed when you are in your own strongest state, have written out your goals and recorded them. When you listen back, it helps push out the old negative thoughts that play in your head all day long. We all have those. "I'm not good enough. Who do you think you are? I'll never achieve that. I'm too fat. I'm too skinny. I'm too old. I'm never going to make it." Much better to replace those with all of the positive things that we know and can create about ourselves, such as, "I am worthy. I am powerful. I am a creator. I am fun and exciting. I'm in a great, healthy relationship. I have valuable intellectual capital. I'm a spiritual being having a human experience. I am fit and healthy. I am positive and loving. I attract all great and wonderful things."

I still do these exercises to this day. I've been doing this for easily 30 years. I believe the efforts of writing things down, having the goals, putting it on paper, and doing audios and videos, are quite powerful.

I would highly recommend taking it to the next level by holding yourself accountable to those goals and dreams by choosing to get some type of a mentor, coach or vision partner to keep you on the right path. The power of accountability is what makes all the difference in your success. And remember, anything you can track and measure, you can improve upon.

An easy way to remember the intent and approach to your goals is the SMART technique. Renowned business and thought leader Peter Drucker spoke of this often. Goals must be:

S – Specific

M – Measurable

A – Attainable

R – Relevant

T – Time bound

Golden Nuggets

 Look for seeds of opportunity in your world day-to-day.

 Write down your dream over time as your thinking about it evolves.

 Make specific plans to begin carrying out various aspects of your dream.

 Use the power of writing, audio and video to drive home your own goals.

 Anything you can track and measure you can improve upon.

Chapter **5**
How the Numbers Fit the Dream

   Many entrepreneurs, creative thinkers and people who dream a lot do not always have a personality style that includes a strong analytical side. I know that we all have a right brain (more creative thinking) and a left brain (more analytical) and we've got to use both sides, but many of us at birth were given a much stronger tendency for skills related to one side of the brain over the other. Some people are very analytical. They think and organize their world on the basis of numbers. They like numbers, sequencing, facts, projects, systems, to-do lists, and blueprints of things.

Other people prefer to fly by the seat of their pants. They operate from emotion and like to go with their gut, go with the flow. They like to just be in the moment. They don't like to make calculated decisions. They use their instinct instead. This is more of a right brain tendency. Sometimes they are two distinct and different personalities. Sometimes people are blessed and lucky enough to have integrated both, so they are able to both understand and manage analytical information, and also be in touch with their gut instincts. There is an equal balance of both in the way they operate, and that is a nice gift to have. If you don't have both, I do find that there is a way to exercise the side of the brain that doesn't come as easily for you.

If someone is very analytical, there are ways to pull them out of their shell and get them into more creative thinking. This may be through workshops, team/group meetings, or perhaps challenging them to do some creative writing as part of their job description. It could be putting them into an environment at leadership events where they are challenged within a group setting to first get comfortable within that group, and then possibly larger groups. You might have them do exercises that can encourage creativity and thinking, dreaming and getting out of the box, and thinking big. We all know that sometimes discomfort leads to forced or chosen growth. As an example, I recently attended a writer's workshop with my wife. She is more right brain than I am. Half of the class consisted of writing short stories and getting feedback from the group, as well as doing improvisations in front of the group. Boy, was that uncomfortable for me! But it really pushed me to be more creative in my writing.

I have been to many, many workshops and seminars with people like Brian Tracey, John Assaraf, Tony Robbins and Marshall Goldsmith. They do things to help people get out of their comfort zones, to stretch oneself to the possibility of 'what if'. What if this could be? What if this could be created?

My assumption at this point is that you have a dream in your mind. You may have a dream already in motion, and you know you want to create even beyond what you already have manifested. Or maybe you are at the beginning stages of creating a dream, company or new job. You have a product or service in mind and you are trying to create that dream. This can be very compelling for people who have an "ah-ha" moment, a prompting or a calling, or just something that has been in their gut for a long time. It could be that your dream has already been birthed, but now you want to grow or change it. And in some cases you may want to bring it to an end. Following that particular mission is sometimes as challenging as creating one. Letting go of a dream is tough, but the same principles can apply.

Numbers as Language

The hard part is usually figuring out the necessary steps to turn your dream into a concrete step-by-step blueprint and having the numbers in your plans supporting your dream. The numbers can help you structure your business growth for investors and maybe partners. If you are raising capital or just want to know what your monthly numbers are, this will help you rank and create success measurements within your dream. Creative and artistic right brain people, who seem to not have the analytical skills that would naturally draw them to appreciate numbers, can be trained to build that muscle.

The process of training yourself to understand how the numbers can help build your dream is a very important piece to have. First, get your head around why that is so important. Let me underscore that. I do believe that anything you can track and measure, you can improve upon. Anything that you can show in numbers or a formula helps explain the concept to others when they are skeptical. It helps you in putting together pro forma's that show you how realistic or unrealistic it is to scale up your dream into something that is actually making money. I say this because we all have dreams. We may want to change the world. We want to make a difference. We want to make an impact. We want to help people or society. At the end of the day, you have to be self-sustaining. Your business needs to be able to make a profit to keep it sustainable, so that it can grow and stay healthy.

It is also a symbol of success. Wealth, abundance or an increase in profit shows you how your dream is being translated into business language and into the public arena. It reflects how your dream is translating to your consumer base, and with your employees and your salespeople. It is very important to know the numbers so that you can track them. If you have ever watched scientific documentaries on television or on the Internet, everything is made up of numbers and everything has a formula. Numbers were a key tool when Einstein created $E=MC^2$ or for any scientist who comes up with theories or mathematical equations. It's the numbers that describe how it works, and formulas tell the story.

Everything on the internet that looks fancy and snazzy, using text, images or videos, is created by sets of numbers that tell your computer what to display on your monitor. Numbers themselves really are the core basis of what the world is made up of in formulas, calculations, and in understanding how we use the language of numbers to translate our ideas into a depiction of reality. In turning your dreams into a reality by using the numbers, realize that in this way, numbers are compatible with your dream. Numbers are simply another language that conveys your dream in a different way, which helps you and others understand the value or benefit of making your dream a reality. And that's telling your story.

I have seen my past coworkers, whether it was real estate agents, business owners, or people wanting to start new divisions or new companies, come with a great, wonderful dream. When I start asking questions such as: "What does this translate into for the benefit of others? How does that work? How many units will you sell in the first year? The second? The third? What kind of profit does that generate? How many people do you plan on reaching? How many calls do you need to make to reach that many people? How many website hits do you need to get in order to convert that into a potential customer? What is your advertising budget?" Many times people do not have those answers. If they understood the numbers to the level of their excitement and enthusiasm, they would have been much more able to convince me to support their dream or proposal. In order to sell this dream to the right people, they needed to develop their ability to go from the dream in their mind, to their speech, to their actions. If you are recruiting people, hiring sales people, starting a business, acquiring consumers and clients to buy, it is important to be able to articulate your dream.

Selling With Numbers

I want to highlight the benefit of understanding how a dream can be sold to someone. There are many times when I was a CEO or a business owner/entrepreneur and one of my managers or a sales person would come to me and share their excitement and enthusiasm about their dream. I would sit and listen to them with interest, but had no clear way to support them because they offered only their enthusiasm and initial ideas. Other times I would have someone else come and they would not only have that excitement and enthusiasm about their dream, but also a business plan to back it up. They would actually have numbers and calculations, and many of the things I mentioned above. They would have needed to show me a written business plan that spelled out some of those overall numbers, timelines and analytical projections.

This got my attention, and made me take even more notice of them. I knew that the person who was taking the time and making the effort needed to put projections and numbers to paper was more likely to succeed. I could see that they believed enough in their dream to put some hard work into it. It made me realize that if they are willing to do that just to get the initial meeting or to get approval from a CEO, maybe this was a good sign. It looked plausible to me that they may have the energy and the know-how to take it to the next level. My belief in them is even further reinforced if they are asking for ideas, and if they are asking for help to get that dream off the ground.

I had one manager who I will call Nancy, who came to me because she wanted to expand her office. She wanted to add additional square footage, and add employees and agents. She wanted to do a remodel and to possibly add another location. There were many times over the years that Nancy came to me and pitched her dream and why she needed what she needed. Having more than done her homework, she would come in prepared. She was more heavy left brain than right. First she would sell me on the dream and the vision, and then she explained the benefits, what people were going to feel or receive from using this particular item, or why the dream had merit or importance. Nancy went on to describe where we should be spending time, energy or money on this particular project and then she would flow into her numbers. She would sit down with me and go over the previous history of the division or the company or that department. I would usually see a 1-2 year history on the progress so far in that particular existing operation. Last, Nancy spelled out what the next six months to a year could look like if we made these potential future investments.

I sometimes looked at this as an investment because I knew there would some type of quantifiable return. But sometimes I looked at it as an expense, which we all know is when you are parting with money. It's just a cost and you don't know how you are going to get a return on it. With an investment, you have a time period on the return, so you know you are going to get your money back, and perhaps a respectable return on your money.

Understanding whether a particular cost is an expense or an investment is always key. People who are really smart when pitching their dreams and their visions and understand these numbers, constantly talk along those lines. They keep the conversation focused on: 'What's in it for the next person? What's in it for the consumer? What's in it for the company? What's in it for the investor? What's in it for the business owner? What's in it for the sales person?" They know what the return is going to be and how long that is going to take.

Nancy always laughed and joked. She was a great storyteller, and great at selling her vision and dream. She was always very prepared with her numbers. There were many times I would push back on her numbers and give her a razz about them, saying one number looked too lofty, or another number was not realistic, or hadn't we already seen this number so why did she have that number so low and why was she sandbagging? I would always kid her about sandbagging her numbers, sometimes keeping them too low versus too high, because I knew she could knock it out of the park. Long story short, by the time Nancy and I had finished our meeting, I knew that she, more times than not, would get what she was asking for.

It became a running joke. Whenever I had a meeting with Nancy, I knew she might be asking for something. I realized as I walked out of our meeting that she probably could have saved herself time, energy and money by giving me a quick phone call, email or a quick summary. I had come to respect her track record and her history so much that I knew if she was pitching it to me, it was probably going to be a good idea. I enjoyed the interaction with her, and the energy and the exchange of the ideas we kicked back and forth was fun. Many times I did bring up issues, topics and ideas that she thought were valuable, and she would modify the dream. Furthermore, she gave me a different perspective or energy about the dream. Having that experience was just as enjoyable for me as it became for Nancy when we bantered back and forth like a good tennis match. You always want to make sure that you are playing tennis with someone who keeps you on your toes and makes it a really fun exchange. Both players get even better.

Selling Without Numbers

I worked with another manager. Let's call her Susie. Susie was very vivacious, outgoing and energetic. She was very much a people person and always wanted the next shiny thing. She was always looking at the next opportunity that would make this the best thing ever. I can tell you that she would come in as enthusiastically with her dream and selling it, but very rarely did she ever have a specific set business plan. She normally had no numbers, projections and returns related to her idea or goal. If she did, they would be too general. Those meetings were usually fun and enjoyable from a bantering standpoint, but these were not nearly as productive as Nancy's meetings. We exchanged ideas and had a lot of fun pushing back and forth, just like I did with Nancy, but the difference was that most of the time I knew the answer was probably going to have to be "no." I also knew that she would most likely have a lot more homework to do before she got a yes. Her personality style and being right brained made it much more challenging for me to get her to take the initiative to come more prepared. She came a little more prepared each time because she knew that I was looking for it.

Sometimes I would say, "Don't come to the meeting without having X, Y, Z," but many times in the meeting she would say, "Oh I didn't get that done" or "I forgot it" or "my dog ate my homework." It was part of her habit, of her personality. She did get better over a period of time, and she did learn to flex and build that muscle, but it was never as ingrained and natural as it was with Nancy. I think this is a big part of our right brain / left brain tendency. I had to really work with Susie to make sure that if I saw value in what she was pitching and thought it had merit, I would sometimes do a little extra homework myself to get that over the hump. But I will be honest, many times I didn't. I was on to my next thing, my next meeting, and my next project. So her ability to sell her dream and make it a reality became much less viable without a clear business plan with numbers.

If you take these two types of individuals, one was prepared on the vision, dream and the numbers, and one was just prepared on the vision, enthusiasm, and excitement and only on the partial steps on the numbers. You can do the math and assume the outcome. You can see which one got what they wanted more than the other. The habit with which you approach business may also be similar to the way you approach life. Whether this is for personal, business or any type of future gain it's important to be clear in how you approach the conversation. Beyond the ability to have a dream, know how to materialize the dream. It's important to encompass all of the tools such as affirmations, writing down goals, putting in step-by-step processes, measurements and matching it to your dream.

Graphing the Numbers

Computer programs are available today such as Excel and many others that will do a lot of the math for you and make it very easy to start graphing, charting and looking at numbers. See if you can graph how $2+2=4$ can actually become $2+2=6$ when you're pitching to someone for a projected return. See if you can put that in a very clear, concise, and well thought out manner that has a step-by-step process. Most people want to see that by months and years, depending on how big this dream is. They want to see how this is going to ramp up in various different measurements and what those key categories would be.

From a business standpoint some of these items are:

- Number of clients

- Number of product sales (which are called units),

  and sales volume, which is the total dollar amount of

  all the units x each sales price.

- An itemized list of all of your expenses monthly and annually.

- Does it save any measurements of time on assembly line or employee cost, getting things faster and more speedily to the consumer, or does it cut out and save any processes?

- What is the startup investment capital needed?

- How long a period is the payback and return?

- If the factors are favorable, how does this calculate into hardcore dollars and cents that save you time and money?

- How will this look to an employer, investor, business owner or an entrepreneur?

When you look at these things and what they are doing for you and your business, it may very well help you accelerate how quickly you want to get things done. When you start looking at the numbers you can see clearly and how rapidly these things can ramp up. You may see a huge return that could even get you more enthused about your dream, your mission and your passion.

It might also encourage other people to get on the bandwagon with you earlier in the game. This in turn helps give you even more momentum, energy, enthusiasm and excitement around that dream. We all know that when momentum starts happening, it is very hard to slow that down. Inertia and the laws of gravity tend to hold things back. But once on a roll, watch out. Something in motion tends to stay in motion and something at rest tends to stay at rest. How do you get your project from being at rest or just in your mind so that it slowly starts rolling? You want it to turn it into a massive snowball that starts rolling down a hill and gains its own momentum, scope and size. How do you gather that much speed? I believe you do that by combining your dream and your vision with your numbers. Your calculated step-by-step approach shows how it is going to benefit someone besides yourself. Show how it is going to make a long-term difference that is attainable, achievable and measurable. Get buy in support, and launch.

Raising Capital

Typically, people first become clear about the offering and product they want to create. I find that before moving forward it is crucial to also get clear on the business side so that you understand the projections and the cash flow that this business will create. It is crucial to know what it is that you are going to be committing to as you go out to create this business. Then you will be able to create a story around these numbers. This will help you create your mission statements and vision statements, and your value proposition. As you are selling to investors, banks or other interested parties, and you get into your story, you are going to want to create a business plan, executive summary, PowerPoint and handout. This document has all of these items in it. Make sure, however, before you present an executive summary for anyone to read, that you have them sign a confidentiality or nondisclosure agreement if appropriate to the product and situation.

Reading a good business plan with an executive summary and a pro forma is like reading a good book. It has a beginning, middle and end. You have highs and lows, some of which peak in that book. And it's a story that keeps people riveted. In the executive summary you create for your business plan, you want to be able to tell in opening stories the overview of your plan and your mission. You want to have the guts and meat of this, which is your business plan, pro forma and budgets.

Elements of an Executive Summary and Business Plan

The main items to address in a business plan are as follows:

1. Business Concept. Describe the business, its product in the marketplace, and why it might have a competitive advantage.

2. Financial Futures. Highlight the important financial points of the business investment.

3. Financial Requirements. Make sure you're very clear about the capital needed to start this and the equity,

if any, that will be provided in funding. You will also need to note any source of collateral.

4. Current Business Position. In this section furnish any relevant information about the company, principal owners and personnel.

5. Major Achievements. This section can contain details and developments within the company such as patents, prototypes, key locations, creative, productive development and the results of any test marketing already completed.

Begin the plan and description by revealing the basics about your business. Include information about how investors will profit. Be clear with your market strategies so they are very specific about your market and the demographics you will be serving.

The major key areas to highlight in this plan are:

- Business description.

- How the venture will create a profit.

- Market strategies and defining your market.

- Pricing and pricing structures for your product or services.

- How distribution will be handled from direct sales and beyond.

- Your sales potential, analyzing increases and when.

- Make sure you're really clear about your competition and you've done some research on a competitive analysis in your immediate market or in your product segment.

- Competitive strength grid.

- Two columns showing weaknesses and strengths. Offer a key category under weakness, and under strengths determine where you stand in relationship. The following categories are useful when you're assessing strengths and weaknesses:

- Product.

- Distribution.

- Pricing.

- Promotion.

- Advertising.

- Goals for product development and future improvements.

- Brief analysis of the procedures or processes that are instrumental to the success of your service or business.

- Scheduling and cost.

- Key personnel you need to run this business.

- Risk involved in developing this product.

- Operations and management of the capital requirements for your team.

- Organizational structure chart for your organization.

If you're asking for capital in your plan, this is where you would insert a capital requirements table, including the timing you request for each level of growth for your business.

If appropriate, you would also have a cost of goods table. This will include three key items: 1) material, 2) labor and 3) overhead.

The income statement would be next. It's a simple and straightforward report showing financial performance that reflects the business sales and financial monitors developed, and combining key elements. The balance sheet includes: 1) assets, 2) liabilities and 3) equity.

On the summary page, include a wrap up for what it is you're asking someone to do. Spell out the next logical steps. You may want them to loan you money, become a partial investor, partner or take a loan that converts to equity. You may want them to provide sweat equity to help build your business. This is all spelled out in an executive summary. By the time they are finished reading your executive summary and hearing your story in person or reading it, they have a very clear snapshot of the vision, and what their return is for their time and money. They now know how they could become involved in this business. They understand how scalable and viable this business is, not only for the consumers, but also for the investors who are looking to help you grow and build your business. Ultimately they want and need to get a return. You will find many times that combining your dreams and visions with the numbers and the process will get you the things you desire faster, smoother and more often.

Golden Nuggets

 Being able to present numbers that illustrate your dream can make all the difference in getting the support of others.

 Write your business plan, executive summary and pro forma with your reader in mind. Will they feel your excitement as though they're reading a good book?

 Make sure the numbers are not only easy to understand, but have a logical path, showing obvious returns.

 Make sure your plan addresses how you're going to overcome the objections and the necessary risks.

 Be clear what you need at every level to materialize the dream.

Chapter **6**
Building the Team

If you understand the sales process, you can really magnify the growth of an organization by driving revenue. At the end of the day the more satisfied customers you have, the better products you have so you can up sell to them things they need or want. The higher the price tag, the more power you have to increase value within your business.

It's sometimes much easier to sell a high-ticket item and have big margins, than selling a low-ticket item. However, if you're consistently selling lots and lots of low-ticket items, it can be the best business in the world. It really depends on your business model and what you're looking for. But the experience of selling really is not that different, so when you go through the probing process to uncover the needs, you're supporting what their needs are, with benefits, whether it's for a high ticket or low-ticket item.

If you happen to be in a one on one presentation, once you've questioned with open probes, which are *open questions,* and close probes, which are *close questions,* you go through this artful dance with someone. The dance involves asking questions, hearing what they say, writing it down, making sure you're then coming back and acknowledging that you heard what they said. You're going into the process, which supports their needs, with features and benefits of your particular product or service. You match your benefits to their desired needs and wants.

In those features and benefits you're highlighting something of value that will solve their current needs. As you go through this process, you're going to walk them through it step by step. You will then build a relationship of trust and having them be heard. Once you build trust with someone, it's really magical from there.

Everybody wants to be heard and to be acknowledged. Everyone wants to think and know that they are of value. A great salesperson understands that, not just in their position as a salesperson, but as a human being. Hopefully they sell because they love people, they love the products and services they're selling, they're really connected and they get energy from it. And remember, as Warren Buffet says, "Price is what you pay and value is what you get."

Great Salespeople

Great salespeople get energy from helping people find successful paths to a conclusion, and getting paid on top of it. Believe me, the payment is icing on the cake. Salespeople are definitely driven by revenue and sales. Whether it's the commissions, awards, recognition, happy clients or combination of all of those, salespeople are driven by these factors.

Finding great salespeople is the key that you want to create in your business. Either recruit them or build and grow them by your phenomenal example as a leader. Groom them internally through your training programs. If you are your own salesperson, then be the absolute best you can be, study the sales process and master it.

Recruiting is the main thing that I did as a manager and as an executive. This also got the attention of my owners, other executives above me and the company in general. In my early days, I was a young, aggressive, want-to-grow, drive-revenue kind of manager. This was clear not only in the hotel restaurant business, but became very apparent as I evolved out of that business into the residential real estate business, managing real estate offices after I had sold real estate for a brief time.

I knew what it was like to be a residential salesperson, and to have to put buyers in your car and show property. I knew how to knock on doors to find listings, and about spending my own money on advertising to try and create leads, and to turn seller's into my listings that could be sold. I went through a great training program in-house based on a version of the old *Xerox Learning Training Program*, which was called *Professional Selling Skills. Professional Selling Skills (PSS)* which is still used to this day. It was a great, very structured, phenomenal training program that I used as a sales person, and in later years as a manager. I also used it as a recruiter and as an owner of the company.

Learning International has developed the following guidelines to help sales people learn through role play:

> Probing: When you want to encourage the customer to respond freely, use open probes. When you want to limit the range of the customer's response to a yes or no answer, or to a choice among alternatives that you supply, use closed probes.

Supporting: When you have uncovered and have a clear understanding of a customer need, 1) acknowledge the need, and 2) introduce the appropriate benefit(s) that satisfies the need.

Closing: When the customer gives you a buying signal, 1) summarize the benefits the customer accepted during the call, and 2) formulate an action plan requiring customer commitment.

Handling Skepticism: When the customer expresses skepticism, offer proof.

Handling Indifference: When the customer expresses indifference, probe to uncover unrealized needs.

Handling Objection: When the customer's objection is due to a misunderstanding, 1) probe to confirm the need, and 2) make a support statement to clear up the misunderstanding. When the customer's objection is due to a drawback, 1) remind the customer of benefits already accepted, and 2) if necessary, probe for more unrealized needs using directed closed probes.

The basic premise is that in all conversations in sales, what you are ultimately trying to do is need-satisfaction selling. You're not trying to high pressure or high power anybody into decisions they don't want to make. What you're doing is uncovering what their needs are. You're trying to show how you or your product or service can satisfy those needs.

And in satisfying those needs, you bring them to logical conclusions while moving them through the sales process. You summarize every step of the way, and lead them to the next action steps they need to take to move them through to that final sale.

Along the way you're also overcoming objections. You're handling skepticism, and dealing with indifference when someone doesn't think they need you or they don't need your product. You're getting through this process and you come to a point when you realize that you're starting to get buying signals, where you're trying to get to a close.

I always say the ABCs of closing are "Always be closing" because ultimately that's what people are looking for. They're looking to be guided and led with wisdom and intelligence to bring them to what will satisfy their needs.

Since a very early age as I began to understand sales and the sales process, I never looked at *salesmen* or the *selling process* as dirty words. I wholeheartedly believed I was doing someone a service. While I was waiting tables, bartending, managing hotels or restaurants, managing comedy clubs, managing my children, managing my relationship, I was always selling something.

You are selling your ideas, and getting people to try and understand your perspective. You're selling products or services within a business, whether it's food, houses, clothing, financial services, or these days, widgets on a computer or apps. There's a certain audience that would value it, could really use it and benefit from it. You sell not from where they are now, but you sell into the vision as to how the product or service will make them feel once they have it.

You may be selling life insurance for a family, or a home that their family can live in. Maybe it's surfboards so they can surf and can have some enjoyment. Or golf club memberships for someone who's created success and wants to have an outlet to unwind after a hard day's work. All services and every buyer and seller have some relationship and connection with the right audience.

The Right Combination

The objective is whether you have the right sales people trying to connect buyers and sellers with products and services. Are you or they trained in a professional way? Are they looking after the client and the consumer's best interest? Do they connect needs with benefits?

If you can tie all of these things together, you really have a magical experience that many businesses have gone on to create. If you look at the experience of companies like Nordstrom, Zappos Shoes or Apple, they are creating a consumer experience that results in customers knowing they have a great product. Companies want to get top dollar for it, but they also want to make sure that they're creating a better experience for the consumer.

Keep Your Competition Close

Being very aware of other companies you respect and value, even if you're doing something completely different from what they are doing, is tantamount to success. It doesn't really matter. The key is to know who your competition is in the marketplace, and to know who has similar employees or salespeople as you. How do those other companies carry the same functions you have within your company? You may have observed clues through transactions you've been in with these companies and salespeople. You may know them because of their reputation of the industry or may have met them at social, business, or trade events. Really getting to know who the key players are in your industry is extremely important. Always strive to do it better and with a 'WOW' factor.

It's just like people who play baseball, football or basketball. They know all of the players of all the other teams. They know their strengths and weaknesses, where they need to grow and learn, and they are pushed by that. They're usually pushed by greatness and excelling. I don't believe that's any different in business, or at least it shouldn't be any different. Know your players, learn who they are and learn who could benefit your organization. See what you can learn from them that may make you or your company better. Then target those people if you think they would add to your team. Next, create a campaign of many things to attract talent to you.

Send notes on accomplishments when you see news about them in a trade publication or when you know they have closed a big sale. You may learn they've gotten promotions at work or that they had a great customer experience that you've heard about. Send them a handwritten note acknowledging their greatness.

Also, make in social media and LinkedIn that you are connected with as many people as possible. Keep current with your social network and your business network online. Watch what they're doing. Make sure you're commenting on posts about their family or their children, the trips they've taken or the education in which they're growing. Follow them and be one of their biggest fans. This is similar to you trying to encourage customers to become raving fans of your business. You could invite them to lunch, or just ask them to be open for a cup of coffee. Ask them to explore what their success is all about. Find out what they do and how they do it. Most people obviously like to talk about themselves. If you give them an opportunity over a cup of coffee or lunch and not make it like it's a formal interview, you can just make it like you're getting to know other talented people in the industry. You can say that you respect who they are and would like to learn more about them. Hopefully this is true. Be sincere and authentic within your own style.

Sometimes it may take two or three phone calls before you get in, but you'll be amazed at how often you'll secure an appointment, and that could be the beginning of a relationship. To build even more effective relationships, you will also want to turn to your major employees who know other talented people. If the top tech person in your company, Jason, knows Susan from company XYZ, see if Jason and Susan can get connected over a cup of coffee and have you invited along. Find out what insights you can get from Jason on Susan, and use that to her advantage and your advantage in trying to build a relationship.

You also can check out company websites. Many company websites have bios, recognition and acknowledgements of these employees. You can kudo them and send them updates. It's great to send Starbucks cards and a congratulations note, or send them recognition gifts online through Facebook or other sources.

Another great product you can find online is called SendOutCards. It is a network marketing company that does a phenomenal job with the power of relationship marketing using personalized greeting cards. And in this day of e-mail, everyone still likes to get a personalized greeting card in the mail with their name on it with a special note. They have a great backend database system with reminders for birthdays, anniversaries, and other special days. You can set up a whole campaign that automatically goes out with your special attention of how you want to manage that program. And you can send small gifts appropriate for many different occasions. It allows you to use something like a contact management system, not just online through e-mail, but a physical product. Recognition and acknowledgement of people is really, really essential. This is also a highly viable tool and system to use with all of your key clients. It is one of the best client retention programs I've seen.

On a side note, I also recommend using something like that within your own organization, so you are constantly recognizing birthdays, anniversaries, special projects and goals that have been met. Offer handwritten notes in little tiny gifts, lunches, sales contests and team events where you have team parties. It all goes such a long way towards building the right culture, morale and environment within an organization.

Recruit targeted people by putting them on your list and ongoing database. You obviously want the ideal customer, client, business model, product and service. You also want to keep 5 or 10 core people at the top of your list to add to your team if you are building one. You may be looking at them for various positions including administrative, sales, executive and succession planning. The people you see as most promising for your organization should constantly be on your list in terms of bringing talent into your company.

Protecting Your Culture

The other advantage of this practice is when your employees know that you're out looking for talent and you're always trying to up your company's hand. This is just by osmosis through healthy competition. It keeps people on their toes. It keeps people realizing that nothing is guaranteed and we can't rest on our laurels for long. This is a business, and as the company grows and gets built, you need to look for the best people to perform and get results.

I am sure you are looking to perform in a culture, and in a team that is united and growing together. If you bring people in from outside who can add to the team with their fresh new talent and energy, it always raises the game for everybody else.

I highly recommend that you're very strategic in your hiring process and when building teams. Keep in mind the type of people you're attracting when trying to create a team, and what you're expecting from them. Make sure you have a very clear picture of what you want and don't want, and you're very clear in defining both of these, every step of the way.

In the recruiting process, you're making it one of your main priorities as you initially build your company, whether you're recruiting in the initial stages a partner, a technician, a CTO, or a financial CFO. You're recruiting the right people at the right phase of your company, and you build the base of your company as if you are building the foundation of a home.

Visualize a house being built with a very strong foundation. You take the time to build it deep into the ground with cement and steel and all kinds of strength, so that anything can stand on top of it. As the house construction begins, you're actually seeing the form of the house, the internal rooms, the roof and the lines of the home take shape.

You don't see any of that until the foundation is done. So the foundation of building your team from the very get-go, and then brick by brick and person by person, is a process. As you build one layer on top of another, you will be amazed at how you can go from one employee or salesperson to 5 to 10 to 20 to 100 if you desire. In one of my past companies when I managed and oversaw as a CEO of Prudential, we had almost 5000 salespeople. When I started with that company, we had about 400. Being part of growth from your company or one you work for can be very exciting and rewarding.

When you build something times 10 or more and you're part of that process, it's amazing how things can start multiplying and how it can just gain momentum of its own. *Momentum* is an amazing, amazing thing. You want and need momentum at various stages, and throughout your company's life. You can also use this same thinking and process in building your customer client base. Regardless, building and growing is key in anything related to business.

Michael Gerber who wrote all the E-Myth books about growing and building small businesses talks many times about going from a company of 1 to a company of 1000. He stresses the importance of your vision, your mission, your purpose, your products and your process. I have had the pleasure of meeting Michael numerous times and talking for hours about the importance of teams, growing and momentum. He is one who believes if you are not growing you're dying. In this day and age of the internet you surely don't need to grow in as many people as you did in previous years to scale. But find ways to grow smartly in the right areas just the same.

Nurturing Your Team

For now, find your talent. Bring them in. Make expectations high. Keep them accountable, keep them rewarded, recognize them, make them feel of value and pay them well with incentives that keep them focused and motivated on the task at hand. You want their attention focused on serving the customer. You want their efforts to improve your company and the environment in which you serve.

It is very important to build a quality team. Clearly, no business ever thrives or grows without a team. I have worked with many teams along the way. In the restaurant hotel industry, I worked with teams of waiters, bartenders and hospitality staff. This actually became one of the best training grounds for me in terms of understanding about customer service. I learned to anticipate the needs of a client or a customer before they even knew exactly what they wanted.

As a waiter I would always be able to predict whether people were going to have wine or cognacs or desserts after dinner, or order extras. I could entice them with my glowing description of the item I was selling to them.

I realized back then I was selling service. I was selling an atmosphere. I was selling an experience. I was selling food and drink. I was really selling a feeling in that whole process. The way I presented and sold this reflected in my results at the end of the night, measured by how many tips I made. I usually did very well.

I also enjoyed serving people, helping them and making them laugh. I enjoyed making them feel like they had a great, unique experience. So at a very young age I learned the art and essence of service, and the uniqueness that one individual can bring to an experience for a consumer.

It's been said before, but it's worth saying again, that one employee, one salesperson, one executive can completely change in a very positive way perspectives and perceptions of a company. They can also kill it as easily, and as fast. I'm sure you've seen this in your own experience. We all notice how people affect us in either a positive or negative way. This happens in your daily course of living, and in all the products and services that you've experienced and have bought over the years.

Taking an average customer experience and turning it into an exceptional memorable experience is truly an example of turning '*Lead to gold.*'

Nurturing Your Customer

What's the difference between a good salesperson and a not-so-good salesperson? What's the difference between a great customer service person and one not-so-good? What makes people want to go to Nordstrom versus a standard department store? It usually is that extra 'something' about service.

It's about making someone feel extra special. It's making them feel they are important. It is making them feel and understand that their needs are your top priority and that you're doing it with enthusiasm, you're doing it with *gusto.* You're doing it with a sense that you're almost participating in the experience with them. That is what really makes the difference. There are definitely people who go through the motions. They're polite and nice enough to answer your questions. But you can always tell when someone is going that extra mile and when their heart is in it.

It's really hard to describe heart. I think that the very best way for me to sum up heart is: It happens when you feel someone is there with you in the moment, enjoying that moment as much as you are and as authentically as you. They're experiencing that process with you, with joy and seeing it through your eyes. And you can feel and understand that they're genuine and truly care. Their uniqueness of being authentic with you is really the intangible.

It's hard to teach employees that, so you have to figure out how to create the environment in which employees can thrive in that mutually shared experience. You also have to realize when you hire people, screen them and bring people in, it's critical to make sure they fit in with your culture. It's critical to make sure they dress appropriately for your business, show up on-time, interview well, that they're prepared, and have great references. But most of all make sure that they're excited and enthusiastic, and that they have a phenomenal attitude. Are they happy and joyful? I've said for years that you don't necessarily hire the wrong people, but you keep the wrong people. If you are not the person doing the hiring but actually you are one of these employees or sales people being hired and working, do your best to embody all being discussed here.

Managing Your Team

Let's say you've done a great job of going through the process of hiring, but you realize you made a mistake, or you want to hang on to someone too long, or you think you can fix someone. People can rarely be fixed. It doesn't mean that people can't be trained if they're coachable and they want to learn. But changing someone's behavior, attitude or love for something is extremely difficult to accomplish and it very rarely happens.

Building a great team and understanding the importance of customer service are keys for any business. This clearly goes back to first understanding your ideal customer. You need to be able to write out exactly what that demographic is. You need to know what kind of person typically would want to buy your product. Who would be attracted to your product? What is the ideal group of people you are marketing to as a client or as a group?

Once you understand your ideal customer and your ideal client, then it's important to also understand your ideal employee and your ideal team. I highly suggest that you write this out and describe it clearly. Not just a job description, but really as an experience. Write out the experience of operations people, sales people, staff people, and marketing people, as if you are able to do all of those positions as an owner yourself or an operator of the company. Make sure to keep in mind the message of what you want your business to be all about, so this permeates the entire experience through people within your company.

When you have the details written out, include them as part of the interviewing process. Include them as part of your staff development plan. Encourage those topics as questions and answers discussed back and forth with management or leadership in the early process of interviewing. Make sure that people are clearly a fit. It's much better to take longer to hire and screen people, than it is to hire people and have to continually train them and turn them over when they're not a fit for your business. You don't know how many good people who do fit that you're losing along the way, if you hold onto someone who is just an okay fit. Perhaps you're holding onto a family member who needed a job, or a friend for whom you're doing a favor. We all do that in running businesses. I've done it myself.

That said, many times those particular individuals don't do you any extra favors. They are not part of your model in thinking and culture, and they don't always fit in. If you hire them and they are not the best fit, it will do more damage to your customer, your business, your morale within your own environment, with other employees, and other people you're trying to attract.

My suggestion is to hire slowly, train deeply, swiftly and long. Expect this will be an ongoing process. You can hire great attitude and teach skills, but it's very difficult to hire someone who has great skills and teach them a great attitude. It's almost impossible. If the choice is between two candidates, go for attitude and heart every single time.

The Alchemy of Creating Your Team

One way of interviewing is where someone meets with different people within your organization. Everyone interviews differently. Everyone interacts with various personality styles differently. It's a good idea to include someone from the marketing side, the administration side or the operation side. All should meet with those key individuals, no matter how small or large the position. It shows the potential employee and potential team member how important this position is, and what the potential is for upswing. And it shows the other team members and leaders within your company that their opinion matters, and that you value their insights and their wisdom. Take their advice and wisdom into consideration when you make decisions for the company. If you're going to ask for it, take it and put it into your analysis when hiring these particular candidates when you're looking to fill certain positions.

Matching Position and Personality

There are many types of personality tests available such as the DISC Process or the *Platinum Rule*. I don't really look at them as a test as much as an explanation of the inner being of that person as revealed by questions that they answer. These questions that are very well thought out and very scientific to draw out the most common denominators in various personality styles. Better yet, you can use an outside service or system that specializes in these skills to help you screen out and select the right candidates.

In building a company, you clearly are going to want one personality style for your sales and marketing team and you will probably want a very different personality style with different values to handle the daily work in your accounting or your legal department. As you're hiring, make sure you clearly understand what type of personality styles you're looking for in each division of your company. These personality surveys, tests or experiences are a great way to also underscore your feeling about this candidate, or the input you get from other individuals in your company.

I highly, highly recommend that you take time to do these personality matches. As you're promoting within your company, you can use this same process when elevating and promoting people within. When you're in a hiring process, it's very important to know how to target the people you're looking for. Stay focused on your 'ideal hire' that you first created on paper from the get-go and then stay focused and match to the actual person.

Finding Talent

Obviously the mode of attracting people has dramatically changed from the days of using print newspapers or publications in your local market like the *Penny Saver*, or bulletin boards on college campuses. These things can still work and be used. What is most valuable and effective is obviously using the power of the Internet and advertising online, whether you use job sites, social media postings, or through target demographic marketing online via social media sites like Facebook or LinkedIn.

Targeting your candidates as to the type of people you're looking for is crucial. My suggestion, as you write your initial ad, is to describe in a very detailed way the type of individual you are looking to hire, along with a brief description about the job itself. More important than the job itself is the personality you're looking for, and what type of belief systems you're radiating in this particular ad and position. You'll be amazed with the number of resumes that come in.

Make sure you're very clear about what you're asking them to submit to you besides just a resume. Are you looking for a video where they can introduce themselves? Are you asking for letters of reference to be provided within the initial resume process? Should you ask them to complete a brief online survey with 5 or 10 questions even before you meet with the candidates? You can also do a quick Skype interview before you have a personal one-on-one interview because you can learn a lot that way as well.

Going through this screening process will save you a lot of time in narrowing down your candidates to the appropriate people that you're actually looking for. Have those candidates that you've drilled down to go through many layers before they're actually hired. Once they're hired they'll start taking resources and training before they're able to add back to your business by serving customers and the consumer.

This method has been proven by businesses that make it and those that don't make it. Businesses that grow and build have shown that taking this time and effort is crucial to building a strong team in the early years and for all of the years ahead.

The other major effort for executives or employees is using a very viable head hunting service. Many of these companies have gotten amazing results if your company budget can afford it. Also consider word of mouth and referrals, which is probably one of the most valuable methods. You can turn to key people you know from your past business dealings, or past experiences and connections.

If you have a relationship with these particular individuals, you have a history and you know something about their background. You know their work ethic, how they get along with others, how they value their workloads, their productivity, and the value of their product. My suggestion is to first go to anybody you've worked with in the past, as you're looking for potential candidates who might fit into one of your open positions.

However, I must emphasize that you do not just hire them because it's easy, quick and convenient. Just because it feels like a great old pair of jeans that fit you perfectly, doesn't mean they fit your company and the particular position you're hiring for. I still suggest you look at outside candidates as you're entering into these decisions because you may find new talent and new blood. It may be more valuable to bring a different energy and different talents than what these known entities have.

The mix of these together is like the alchemy of great chemistry and formula of hiring a team. Consider factors such as enthusiasm, specific skills, experience, attitude, cooperation, collaboration, knowledge base, can-do attitude, and being open to growth. Weigh the importance of how those fit into your hiring choices, and how this builds upon your existing team. Will it add or deplete the team you already have?

Go through your past experiences and relationships in business, and ask your respected family, friends and business associates of people that they know for referrals. You can do that through social media, phone calls, through an e-mail campaign, and various other sources. Collect referrals of friends of friends because then at least you have one more degree of reference than you would than from someone who came straight from an Internet ad.

The other point I would make is to get into recruiting from other companies. Many industries in sales actively go out and seek talent from other companies. They market and basically lure them away. That's the best way to put it. Having been in the real estate business for 25 years, I know it was a very common and accepted practice that recruiting and luring talent from other competitors was the way companies were built, grown and diminished. This happened to me over my career and as a business owner many, many times. I have been on both ends of the coin.

If you realize this is how the game is played in your industry, then swallow that pill and make yourself and your company the best at doing this, above and beyond the competition. This needs to become part of your ongoing mission in seeking and growing talent within your organization. The chemistry of building teams can be organic, hiring from scratch, grooming from within, or, as stated, luring talent from competitors. The bottom line is you have to continue to grow and increase the quality of your talent and people within your company in a never-ending fashion.

Golden Nuggets

 Develop a good understanding of

the sales process.

 Find sales people who truly enjoy helping other

people get what they want.

 Keep tabs on what your competition is doing.

 Know the culture you want your organization to

reflect.

 Nurture your team and your customers with that

culture in mind.

 Remember that you don't necessarily hire the wrong

people, but you keep the wrong people.

Chapter **7**
Products and Branding

If you are creating a brand from scratch, there are many questions to ask yourself and your team as you're positioning your brand. In addition to soul-searching, it will also involve doing some market research, a competitive review, and a brand audit identifying what you're trying to accomplish. What's already in the marketplace? What strategy will best meet the needs of your potential customers, and your needs as a company?

What are you trying to portray to the consumer from your brand? How are you going to do that? Is it relevant to them? Is the product you're branding something the consumer needs? How do you know the consumer needs it or wants it? Is it relevant in this day and age, or is it obsolete?

From your point of view, what message are you trying to convey? Is it a personality brand? Is it a product brand? Are you trying to stimulate a higher-end feel, a middle market feel, or an affordable, cost-effective feel?

So as you look at these, think of the other attributes, value propositions and promises that competitive companies and brands are creating for their products and services. What are you competing with? What is already being offered in the marketplace? Are you planning to do it better, faster, cheaper, or more exclusively in a higher luxury format? How are you planning to deliver the product or service that's different from your competitor?

Doing your homework of review, market research, brand audit, competitive review and discovery is important. If you're the one leading and driving the company, plug into your own heart and personality. What is it that you're already projecting in your company?

Some of this information will also be pertinent if you're already an existing business and running a company. If you have already started a brand you may be looking for an update. You may be looking to maximize your sales by having a different messaging around your brand. Or you may be starting a brand from scratch.

You may be constantly asking, "Is our branding (not so much our logo and our colors, but the messaging around our branding) still relevant?" Today when so much has gone digital and online, it's very easy to update and fine-tune the NLP language and copywriting around our branding and messaging. NLP is neurolinguistics programming, which is essential to building a compelling message to convince people to buy your product or service, or to want them to work with you. NLP is a connection between specific words and language that prompts the brain and emotion to act or relate in very specific intended ways.

Prudential had 98% name recognition on its brand and on its logo when I worked with them. This means that 98% of Americans knew when they saw the rock, the Rock of Gibraltar, what that meant. And for many years, their logo or slogan, 'a piece of the rock' was associated with the peace of mind people wanted. Since the company was built on investments and insurance, and providing people with safety and security from catastrophe, or to make sure they were set up for retirement or for savings, that was a very good slogan in that day and age of preparing for security and safety.

Prudential branded themselves around the Rock of Gibraltar, which is a huge rock at the end of the Iberian Peninsula, separated from Morocco, North Africa, by the Straits of Gibraltar. It was a big symbol as to what Mother Nature can do to produce something of such magnitude that is so strong and is so stable. It stood the test of time and withstood weather. It continued in its strong formation. For Prudential, they thought this was a great brand logo. They've changed the image over the years many times. If you looked at the history of the hundred years of the Prudential brand, it has different colors and different fonts, but the Rock of Gibraltar was always the center of it, even when they changed their tag line.

Doing Your Homework

You can look at current companies that have come out in recent years. Think about how long *Google* has been around. If you look at their history, it definitely has not been a hundred years. Look at Mercedes or even in the real estate business, Zillow, or at Starbucks. When you look at these brands and how they've evolved over the years, you'll notice they do their homework. They know what they're trying to portray, what type of emotion they're trying to evoke from the consumer, what their product is, and what market they're going after. As you're looking at your business, it's key that you look at all those things, and do your homework well.

In the discovery stage you will want to review all of the existing materials you have right now. Gather all the input you have and have it ready in front of you, so that you and your team can assess it. You will be doing market research whether you're starting up or you're new. If you're brand new, you may not have a lot of materials to review unless you're pulling from your competitors' materials. You can print what you find online or the brochures, magazines or information you've collected from other sources.

As you begin your brand audit, look at your brand right now, while holding a clear picture of your mission statement, your core values and your purpose in mind. All of those have an important part of your brand audit research.

Competitive review is also important. Who do you consider your top five competitors? What are they doing and saying about themselves and the marketplace? Look at their sites, marketing, messaging, colors, fonts, slogans, imaging, videos, and their photography.

All of those activities are part of Phase I. In Phase II you can start exploring, defining and really crystallizing the strategy and brand positioning in a couple of key areas. How are you going to position your brand? Where are you going to do it within key market areas? Are you going to do it online, print, direct mail, or a combination of all of them?

Value Proposition

Next, what are your value propositions? What is the offer that you're putting through as to what your value is to the consumer? The old acronym, WIIFM—and no, it's not a radio station (we don't even really listen to radio stations as much as we used to. Podcasts seem to be the new medium in that space), WIIFM in the sales and marketing business has always stood for, "What's in it for me?"

The consumer, when you're talking with them, when they're reading your materials, watching a video online, seeing you on Facebook and reviewing your website, in a few seconds your customer is questioning in their mind, scanning the information and looking for, "What's in it for me? Why would I care about that?"

You want to make sure that as you're coming up with the clearest information about what your value propositions are whether you're selling shoes, clothes, food, consulting services, Internet services, social media services, or men's watches. Whatever you might be selling, be sure to define the proposition and the value to the consumer.

Brand Attributes

What are the attributes of your brand? What does your brand attribute its messaging around? What are the core values of the brand? What attributes does it have? Think of this as though you're describing somebody's personality. Are they funny? Are they witty? Are they smart? Are they intelligent? Are they brutish? Are they quick? Are they slow? What are some of the attributes of a person that matches the brand you want to offer?

What is it that you value? Do you value great service? Do you value phenomenal pricing? Do you value a shorter amount of delivery time? Do you value ethics and professionalism?

Most of all of the things above are part of what any company would want, but it's important to drill down and figure out how to make the words as creative as possible. Come up with some unique, highlighted items that you completely value as a human being, as a spiritual being and as a business leader. How do you take those values and add them within your own brand messaging?

The best thing to do is to write them down on a piece of paper or on your iPad. Start writing the words that represent the image you're trying to portray. Let your graphic design artist and branding specialist help you figure out how to get that across in images with the feel you envision.

Brand Promise

What is your brand promise? What will you deliver? How are you going to make sure the product or service is delivered to the consumer? What is your promise to make sure they're going to be happy?

Do you have a money back guarantee? Do you have a trial period? Do you have testimonials from happy clients? Have you had very few customer complaints? The promise is delivery and that you have a way to solve any problems that may arise in your process. If you're going to have a promise and if the promise is broken, you typically have some sort of guarantee to build trust so your customers are satisfied.

As an example, if a Starbucks customer doesn't like their drink, they'll make it for you again instantly. Whether it's too hot, too cold, too sweet, whatever it might be, even if it's the way you ordered it and you made the mistake, they'll still

182

make another one for you. They have a brand promise of delivering an experience during the time that you walk into Starbucks, including how the tables are set up, the smells in the café, the imaging on the wall, and the type of service their customers receive. Starbucks has their free little cards they give away if they made something too slowly or if they ran out of something, and they give you a free drink for next time. They have clear a brand promise on how they're going to deliver their product.

They understand the process of turning 'Lead into Gold.' Anytime you can take a challenge and turn it into a valuable opportunity, you are in motion on the '*Lead to gold*' concept. I know consultants who don't get paid until the end of the month or year after the person has been satisfied with the services. My mentor and friend, Marshall Goldsmith, doesn't get paid until after a full year. Marshall does a stakeholder 360° interview of the direct reports that are supervised or report to the CEO or the COO. All of them are interviewed frequently and also at the end of the cycle that this person has been coached. The person being coached and the key stakeholders all have to have agreed that this person has improved in the areas in which they said they wanted to improve.

The brand promise that Marshall gives is that he's going to make sure he gives his best in the intention that the person improves; if they cooperate and do the work. Marshall will put in his time to make sure that he offers all of his skills and wisdom. Then, if the stakeholders and the Board of Directors believe that there has been progress, Marshall gets paid at the end of the year. He has fulfilled his promise. And that's really putting your money where your mouth is.

Not everyone is in the position to be able to do something like that, but offering some guarantee that has feasibility like this is a really strong proposition showing what your values are, your brand attributes and your brand promise.

Brand Position

Next is the messaging matrix on your positioning, which means putting together a visual representation as to how the messaging is going to get across. There are so many ways to use messaging. Have great copywriting from text based messages, email, print media, direct mail, magazines, online, digital, skimming banners, pre-roll on *YouTube* and various messages on Pandora or other frequented consumer areas.

Once you're clear on the positioning of your brand, how are you going to break in and make sure that those things are mapped out for deployment?

How do your messages look? Are they visually appealing? What kind of emotion or expressions are you trying to get across within them?

Naming Your Company

It's really worth spending extra time on this. It's almost as if you're planning for and having a baby. You may know how long it takes to pick out a baby's name. You do a lot of thinking about it. You spend a lot of time looking at books, looking online, writing it out, saying it and playing with how it looks with the first, middle and last names. This is important and creates identity, so give it the time due. If you know it in an instant and it rings true, go for it. Use that one.

As you're naming your company and looking at branding your company, think of having your baby brand go from grade, school, middle school to junior high, high school to college. You want it to grow. How would you want that to be seen or show up in the world? Just as you would place high importance on what you're going to name your child, what are you going to name your company? Make sure it can grow and be relevant over time, and that you truly love it!

Spend time thinking of the name, so you have the most passionate and heartfelt feelings around it. Now that you've done some real soul-searching, no matter what the naysayers, haters or bashers say, you can stand behind your company logo and name. Stand up for it just like you would stand up for your child if someone were picking on your kid.

Creative Thinking

As you're working in this creative phase, some of the things you look at as you're inventing or re-assessing a brand is not only the logo, but also an array of logos. Having a great graphic designer give you many choices can be helpful. Choose one that is clean, crisp and current, and also can stand the test of the time. Maybe you want traditional or old world feel. You want to be able to have a logo that is not too limiting in your marketplace, unless that's your specific need and desire.

Some people want to have a very limited niche market, such as women between 40 and 50 who like to travel and ride Harleys. Maybe that's their audience. So they would be very, very specific on only wanting to appeal to that type of group. They don't really care about the rest of the market audience. They're making a very conscious decision.

But if you're a general marketer and you're trying to appeal to the wide masses of consumers, men and women, young and old, the millennials and the baby boomers, then you want to keep that in mind when you're thinking about color palettes, typography, and especially in your photography style and possible use of video.

You also want to consider your communication system, business cards and email templates. How are you going to communicate? Is it electronically? Is it print? And if you're communicating from letters that are being sent out to communicate, how do you want that to look once in someone's inbox or mailbox?

Copywriting

Good copywriting services are also valuable to invest in. Having a great copywriter to help you with your messaging, copy, creativity, your bio on yourself, and the message around the company is key. A good copywriter is worth their weight in gold because the art of language and the written word is really what compels people while they start reading through your messaging.

Now, granted, today's consumer is much less likely to read as much text as they did in past years. Today is much more about the image and a few words that can capture the eye. If they want to look further on, they can click on links and often dig down into as much detail as they'd like.

But if you only have a few words or sentences to grab and get your message across, a great copywriter can be the crucial element in the way the text can portray the personality of you and/or your company.

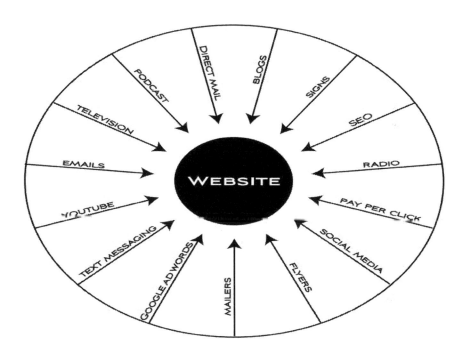

Your Website

Think about your website design. This is probably one of the biggest things that pull all of the elements of content together. To me, the website is like the hub of a spoke and wheel system. Everything has to go back to the web.

If you think about an illustration that is in the middle is your brand and website. Each spoke that comes out would be what supports your website, such as social media, direct mail, magazines, email marketing, text message marketing, banners and signage. Everything, in my opinion, has to come back to the web as the hub of it all.

Your website has to be the key that ties it all together. Every time someone sees a business card, an eblast, Facebook posting, direct mail piece, banner ad … if they click back to your website, everything should be congruent—the look, the feel, the colors. Your web is there 24 hours, seven days a week. It can be accessed anywhere in the world. This is your hub for directing and collecting your consumers' attention and interaction, unless it is live, which of course is best! You want to make sure that your website really reflects the heart and soul of your company.

It is so crucial to make sure that your website gets a lot of time and thought. You're figuring out how simplified you want it, what kind of colors you want and to make it as user-friendly as possible to the consumer. I've looked at many, many websites over the years. I've managed thousands and thousands of real estate people and they all had a company website that we've provided, but 85% of them also had their individual custom websites where they had their own messaging, brands, and client testimonials in addition to properties that could be displayed. Many agents were very creative in what they were marketing, what kind of communities they were marketing to and what they wanted on their own individualized, personal messaging under the company brand. Having lead capture pieces on your site in dominant, compelling ways is crucial.

Find a way to give an offering of some value to collect your clients contact information. You can offer eBooks, free market surveys, free videos, coupons, or assessments. Offer something of value in exchange for their valuable contact information. This will be key in staying in touch and building trust and rapport.

I've also seen many websites over the years from both individual entrepreneurs and larger companies. I've looked at very large institutions and organizations and how their websites were put together and built. In every business consulting session, I've had with executives or with independent contractors or entrepreneurs, their websites have been key. I know this is redundant, but the importance is massive enough to make sure that your website is the hub of everything that you do.

These are the key items you want to look at in the creative stages: logos, color palettes, typography, style, photography and video, email systems, website designs, and copywriting services. Getting these elements right are the foundation for building your marketing and promotional strategy.

Golden Nuggets

 Have a clear understanding of the message you want to convey through your branding.

 Do your homework. Continuously research the market, do a brand audit and competitive review.

 Know what the market values, and match your value proposition to what your customers will buy.

 Be clear about your brand promises, and live up to them.

 Present your brand consistently across promotional pieces, online and offline.

Chapter **8**
Marketing and Promotion

Now that you have it clear in your mind and in your marketing collateral how you want to present your company and your offering, how do you take all of that and produce results? How do you activate a timeline that gets mapped out into execution? How do you make it enough of a high priority with your employees and salespeople to make sure all of these things really get to the consumer and back within the consumer marketplace?

Considering your website or websites, they need to be tied to your social media and cross promote them with each other. In terms of digital marketing, how are you going to advertise online with either banners or Google AdWords or Facebook advertising? Video production becomes a whole initiative upon itself. It does not need to take a lot of time to do great videos. Hiring a phenomenal videographer makes a huge difference. If you can combine video along with your photographer for your still photography, it's great. You could be videoing the entire process as you're building your company. You can be videoing if you're an existing company, documenting how you're going to revamp or remodel. Show scenes behind the curtain if you like. Some of them can be really fun and unique on how companies are building themselves. Use some of that footage as you reinvent yourself for social posts. Using a basic phone or smart phone can work great for more casual, intimate and personal items you are trying to capture and portray. This can work wonderfully in social media, email blasts and company YouTube channels.

Signage

If you're a brick and mortar business, signage is obviously important. In my past life I was in real estate, so signage was huge for us. We had signs not only at each of our brick and mortar buildings, but we also displayed signs in yards, because every house that we had for listing and/or sale was a potential opportunity to advertise our brand. It not only promotes the company, but also additional services and future sales. There are a lot of things you can do with a yard sign that people see as they're driving by. You add flier boxes, special offering and features of your product or service. Thinking in your own business where you may have opportunities to maximize your similar sign opportunity.

If you're not a brick and mortar business, then your signage is on the Internet. Banner advertising is kind of like billboard advertising. Some people currently still use billboards. I live on a quarter intersection of a business/beach community. It's a coastal highway and a quarter where there's tons of traffic. It's right by the ocean. There's a billboard sign there that's constantly full. And it's constantly changing and evolving because people see it so easily. It's a great branding opportunity for people who might have money in their budget for the product or service being advertised.

Packaging

If you have a product, look carefully at your product packaging. If you're actually selling something like a computer or a stationery package, glassware, shoes or jewelry, whatever it might be, what is your packaging? How does it look and feel when someone actually buys it off a shelf from a store? How does it look if they're getting it shipped to their home through Amazon or through your own delivery system?

What is it that they see when they get the package? Is it wrapped in a bow? Is it wrapped in paper? Is it a hard box? Is it soft? What are the colors? Is it easy to open? Is it classy? Is it safe? Consider all those things as you look at product packaging. You want to appeal as best you can to the five senses as you package your podcast, for instance.

Most of the businesses I've been involved with were service oriented, so didn't actually deliver a product. Some companies sell brownies, computer parts or art work. With these products it is really so important to have someone help you with product packaging. Make decisions as to how you're going to package and see that your brand is transferred all the way through to the delivery process. In addition, given today's move to more environmentally friendly and green materials, many people are going with packaging that uses recycled paper or less paper, or no plastic.

Keep in mind the messaging you're trying to get to the consumer. If that's a big part of your business model, don't say that you're environmentally friendly and then send your product filled with plastic wrapping and foam and

Styrofoam. It's overly excessive and kind of defeats the whole message.

Advertising and Public Relations (PR)

Public relations are very different from advertising. And advertising, obviously, is very different from public relations. But public relations is something that, if done well, can get you massive amounts of exposure. As an example, if you get a press release about your business, your company or your CEO in *The Wall Street Journal*, this exposure can be put on blog posts and recycled on social media. The magnitude of having all of this exposure versus just running an ad in *The Wall Street Journal* is priceless. Maximize it in every one of the spokes and hub of the marketing wheel you can to gain more exposure.

Are you going to hire a PR agency? Are you going to do it yourself? If you're going to do it yourself, you should look into a service like PRWeb, which is a service you can buy, that allows distribution of articles online. They'll hit many of the wire services and help you get exposure. It's a monthly package you can buy. It'll also help you on marketing yourself from a PR standpoint for your own personal brand.

Advertising and PR are crucial. When you look at a brick and mortar business, one of your biggest expenses is typically rent (this is of course if less your actual base product cost if you have a physical product). The other large expense in a traditional business is payroll and staffing. Your advertising budget is typically in your top three. So advertising and promotion of your products are the top three budget items in your business. This makes a good case to find a way to make sure you're maximizing your advertising and branding dollars. I don't really think of it as an expense item, even though it shows up on your P&L that way. I've always thought about advertising as an investment.

Advertising is something that people used to think of around print media. They thought of newspapers, magazines, and of billboards. That's all traditional, hard copy marketing. I am not somebody who personally believes that print media is dead. I believe that if print media is tied to the web and to the digital and social world, it can be a great adjunct to your marketing program. If the advertiser with which you're advertising is not tied to all of those things, I don't typically even suggest talking to them.

As an example, our local market here has the *San Diego Union Tribune*. Their paper has gone through many transformations of change in readership, product and scope as many other newspapers have. The newspaper business has been dying, but it's not dead. They did a great job of converting over to the online side in San Diego website advertising. And if you're in their paper as an advertiser, there are many things you can link to from print to web and vice versa.

As a CEO of a company or as an entrepreneur/owner of my own company, I made sure every time I met with my advertising rep who was trying to sell me something, I would tell them not to even start the conversation unless they showed me every ad dollar that I spent in print media was tied to something, whether it was a tweet, Facebook, impressions on their site, additional PR articles I could get online on their website, blog or featured articles that I could do, or videos that I could do within their company. I always made sure that if I was buying something in print media or magazines that I had that conversation with every representative I was talking with. And it's amazing what you can do to maximize your buy to advertising and PR when you're coming from that mindset.

Now, clearly, I understand that many media these days are only digital. They don't even have a print piece. They're completely selling up and marketing up those items. Two of the big disruptors in our marketplace were Zillow and Trulia in the real estate space. If you go to the book business, it was Amazon. If you go to the movie business, look at what Netflix did to the Blockbuster world. Many of these changed dramatically because it's all digital. In that case advertising pricing starts at the level where they're not trying to leverage or maximize the print product. They're really only selling digitally online.

It does work. But during your negotiations and initial buys use the exact same mindset as stated about print. Get perks, bonuses, extra space, PR, social media connections and other options as available. Ask the representative to see every and all options in their arsenal and try to negotiate the best deal for you. This always works best when they are first trying to get you or sell you as a new client.

Local

However, that being said, as a small business owner or a local entrepreneur, there are still many local newspapers and magazines in the local marketplace that still have reach. I live in a series of beach communities in San Diego. From Encinitas to Del Mar, which is about a 10-mile stretch, there are two or three newspapers that cover all those zip codes for that 10-mile stretch along the coast. So many businesses, whether it's real estate, restaurants, cafes or music shops will advertise in those local papers because they want to focus on that local community. They will also leverage themselves to those newspapers that have gone all digital online.

This could be a very good opportunity if you're a small, local entrepreneur. Many people are also advertising on things called *Patch*. A patch is also something that is actually a digital local *PennySaver*, in the local communities. And that's very creative because it's specific to a zip code. See about being sponsored free when they have space to fill, get PR and tie into any time they are promoting local community and business events.

Those are some ways you can look at maximizing and creating some local relationships with people who you're buying print media from, advertising or digital advertising.

Global

If you're a global business covering national or global marketplaces, those local venues are not going to work for you. You want to have something that gives you the biggest scope, depth and reach with the lowest cost, which will give the right impressions to the right consumers and the right-targeted approach. That's why online advertising is so huge, and why companies like Facebook and YouTube have caused the digital advertising world to be turned on its ear. With online marketing, you can clearly target down to age groups, demographics, likes, dislikes, times of day, and days of the week you want to advertise. You can decide when your budget is going to hit a certain number, when it turns off or on, depending on when you're starting to get certain lead responses. There are so many things that you can dial down that really make your ad-buys effective.

Every Penny Counts

Advertising as a small business entrepreneur or corporation is something that takes a lot of thought because there are still many ways to waste money both online and in print. Every penny counts with ad dollars and profits, so you want to make sure you're carefully mapping out your annual plan for your business and then breaking that down on a quarterly, monthly and a weekly basis. This allows you to look at what you have allocated for the year, how you're going to break that down in your advertising cost for these different mediums, and how you're going to track it. I recommend not spending any dollar unless you can track and measure it. Again, that's why the online element is so important. You can do your Google Analytics report each month and find out where all the traffic is coming from. And that's why sometimes print media is much harder to track and scale. One tactic is to put promo codes or ad codes in print media, so when they're going back online to get a discount or to get credit for something, there is a way to track where the source came from.

As you're spending each dollar, map it out annually, quarterly, monthly and weekly. And then break down what percentage you're going to be spending in those particular areas. Give yourself space to be flexible. If you're reviewing things monthly and quarterly, as you're looking at your P&L's and see your results and your capture rates, you can tweak these items. You can ebb and flow. Where you're seeing a big success, you want to maybe turn those up. Where you're seeing zero success, even though you thought it was going to work really well for you, you may want to dial those things down. Focus on turning every dollar you spend on advertising into five dollars, and find a way to track and measure everything.

Also keep in mind that advertising never works out as quickly as we think it's going to. You do need to expect that some campaigns have longer shelf lives. Do test the market versus giving up too soon. Sometimes it takes deeper penetration with the market in order to get the bigger results.

Client acquisition cost is another factor. How much is it costing you to get that consumer from the time you got them to look at your product or service, whether it's in person or online, to converting to a sale? Find a way you can use to start tracking every dollar you're spending, and on the advertising and marketing piece. Track the cost to acquire your consumer from inception to sale.

Low Budget PR

The importance of the PR piece is something that I can't express enough. I'm such a big believer in PR. It's what helped me build many of the offices and divisions within the real estate companies that I ran and owned. And that's also partially how I made a reputation for myself as a real estate and an entrepreneurial leader in the marketplace. I had many, many opportunities to be on the front page, the real estate or business section of the newspaper, because I was being interviewed as the expert. I made sure that I was always available to reporters or people doing research on the market, real estate trends and changes. I made myself available by offering to be available.

I'd show up at networking events and introduce myself to the appropriate people. I made sure that when I was buying products from these different publications, that I included PR as part of my agreement, and that I had the opportunity to be interviewed a certain number of times. One thing you'll find is that many times the advertising division does not connect and talk with the editorial division. It's like the separation of church and state. But there are still dotted lines, so you can still tie into the overall marketplace.

Making sure that you are ready to return a phone call as soon as a reporter calls you within moments is key. Doing your homework, doing your research, sending in articles, making sure that you're submitting articles in either blog posts for *Entrepreneur.com* or *Business Week*, as they're always looking for content, you can see what gets picked up. Making yourself available and reaching out to the people that are already writing in those publications in which you want to be part of, liking their work, giving them kudos and trying to have them become a fan of yours if you're a fan of theirs. Maybe they can get you introduced to editors, and can help you in various ways.

But I cannot express enough the importance of having somebody central within your organization, whether it's you or your marketing person, or it's a position that you outsource, really focus on creating as much PR for new products, new services, employees that you hire, sales people that you hire, community work that you're doing, and new reviews that you have from the consumer. If something interesting is happening in your industry, having PR articles and news is invaluable. You can always link back to your website, your blog, and your Facebook postings.

You can also advertise it. Once you've been noted in a publication, whether it's a video or a television show or a newspaper article, using it in advertising can help you maximize it by ten-fold. The importance of these PR articles is crucial to activating, building and implementing your branding in the marketplace.

Ongoing Monitoring

The thing I want to wrap up with now is ongoing management, evaluating how things are working and fostering your brand over the time. I recommend having somebody with a real creative eye make you accountable about keeping your brand pure and protected.

It's just like you want to make sure that your child, if you have one, is protected at school. If they scrape their knees you want to put a Band-Aid on it and clean it up. It's the same thing with your brand. Have an ongoing, frequent look at your brand and the messaging around it, and have some outside eyes and counsel help you to do that.

You can also do this through customer reviews. You can use Yelp and all of the social media reviews that are out there. Create online surveys and find out how you're doing with your customer service. Monitor how consumers are seeing and experiencing your brand.

Keep some kind of a brand scorecard where you list five or eight items each month that you check about the brand. Is your messaging getting out? Is it clear? Is it in the right font? Is it in the right color? Are they using the right words? Are you getting a response back on it? Are you seeing an increase in communication? Are you seeing an increase in leads coming into the company? Are you seeing an increase in sales? Are you getting the right price points that you want on your overall product? You want to make sure to list items that answer the question, "How am I making sure that this is happening?"

Make sure that you are clearly focused on your own market research by tracking your brand's scorecard and having counsel around your brand. In addition, constantly keep up-to-date on what's happening with your competitors.

I recommend putting your competitor on Google Alerts. Google Alerts are great because everything that gets published online that's an article, a story or something of value is available to you through an email alert, which keeps you updated on what's happening in their marketplace.

You can sign onto their websites for their newsletters and their blog sites. Stay on track about what's happening with your competitors because you want to stay ahead of the game. You don't want to copy your competitors, but you want to know what they're doing and when they're doing it. You want to know when they're zigging, so you can zag.

As we wrap up this particular chapter, I think you'll find that the key is taking time to do your research. Gather all of the input and really position your products and brand into different categories when you can. If you're going to be creative in your process of building and growing your brand, monitor how you activate and implement, and how you manage that in an ongoing way.

One of the biggest things you can do above and beyond all of this once everything is in place is to start gathering customer testimonials. Testimonials are so important. Have incentives and perks for your consumers. Make sure your employees and your salespeople are always soliciting, asking for and being trained from the very beginning to tell the customer that they're going to be wanting to earn the best opportunity through a testimonial, so that they can wow the consumer and create raving fans. Have that part of the DNA from the very first time you meet someone, to the very first time you deliver a new product or service. Maintain the follow up system you have in place that helps you make this happen. It needs to be part of your internal DNA system within your own structure of your own company.

I can't stress importance of testimonials from your employees, your customers and even your competitors go. The testimonials go even further than the PR piece because people believe third-party testimonials more than they believe your own PR.

Those two things combined, testimonials and PR, will be the magic pill that makes all of your branding, advertising and marketing work for many years to come.

Golden Nuggets

 Use all methods of getting your branding messages to potential customers as you can, that fit your market.

 Public relations can be less expensive and more effective than advertising.

 Look at both global and local promotional opportunities, and know how to negotiate for greater leverage.

 Continually monitor how things are working overtime and adjust the course as the data reflects.

Chapter **9**
The Art of Seduction

It is important to keep things as simple as possible with your sales process, while keeping in mind the systems that are a part of any business. What is the DNA or higher purpose/spirituality of any business? By this I mean the workings of input and output. Just as in your body you have your skeletal structure, muscles, nerves and your skin that surrounds all of that, and the blood that flows through everything. The whole organism connected together has to work in harmony to create the human body, and then our spiritual connection ties it into a higher purpose or a Higher Power which gives it the energy or its source for its own creation and creative outlet.

Think of business as its own organism. In business you have people, marketing, sales and systems. In the spirituality of business or in the DNA of a company, businesses are made up of these four components: people, marketing, sales and systems. These are truly the cornerstones of any business. Regardless of what type of business you are running, whether it is a restaurant, hotel, landscaping business, real estate business or a consulting business, these are the cornerstones. Without them there would be no business. If you have great marketing but you have no sales or systems to funnel that through, then your business will not last long and provide the end result you want. If you have great systems and great infrastructure, but you have a horrible marketing program, then your leads and your potential client base are going to be minimal. So they all must work together. The real essence of marketing is the message. What is your message? What is your unique value proposition? How do you describe in as simple terms as possible what the consumer is going to receive? And do they want it?

I recently had lunch with my friend and mentor Brian Tracy who wrote the foreword for this book. I am so grateful to him for that. Also some of the concepts I discuss and share in the book came right from some of Brian's trainings and books. He has been a friend and invaluable to me over the years personally and professionally. Part of our lunch was spent talking about this very thing. You must make sure your products and services are in direct alignment with exactly what your client needs. When you focus on creating or perfecting your UVP (unique value proposition), how do you position that? Brian suggests doing something that just 'grabs them' in with heart and intrigue to have a spark and desire to find out more.

Once you have them find ways to convey your message of quality and high value, Brian says the quality of your offering can be up to 80% of the difference whether you get and keep a client, or if you lose them. Quality clearly matters. Focus on being better and of more value to them in obvious, clear repeatable ways.

Make sure to always remember you and your company are responsible for the quality result you bring about. It is not the customer's' job to try and figure it out. Wow them with service, follow up and creating a 'feel good' process and system. Think of Apple, Tiffany's, Nordstrom's, BMW, LuLu Lemon and create new ways to be of value. Find your niche and your path to being the leader in your own niche.

Be known above all for what you do best! Sell, promote and market that!

So in summary it is as easy as:

1. Make your value offer crystal clear,
2. Who and what segment of the market does it really value, and
3. Create your own clear path as to how you uniquely get to your customer and communicate with them.

The ultimate goal is continuing on a path of quality and value, finding ways to create clients for life.

Hub and Spokes of Your Marketing Wheel

Obviously in marketing you have many arenas to get that message out today. The day of print is not gone, but it has definitely diminished. Any print message must be accessed and highlighted with digital and online media connected to print. You can use print, digital, and online social media, websites and blogs. Search engine optimization can drive traffic to your sites, which is a whole marketing level that delivers the foundation of your marketing messages. In addition, you can use mail that can be delivered to the consumer with your message electronically or in print.

When designing your key marketing program think of a wheel with spokes coming out of the hub. The hub is the core of your marketing program. All of your spokes go out and come back into the center. I see your website as the hub of everything you do. Your presence everywhere else drives traffic back to the website hub of your marketing presence.

What is your sales process? What is your sales message? How do you actually sell what you are marketing? Once you have the opportunity to go through that process and get a consumer connected to you, then you want to be ready to make an effective presentation. How do you open up the conversation? How do you get clear on their needs, and what they are looking for? How do you introduce and create need satisfaction selling? What is the process you go through to overcome skepticism and objections? How do you know when you are getting buying signals? How do you close the consumer to the next relevant step? This can all be addressed in the need satisfaction selling process.

Many times the close is not just the final close of getting the deal closed, but it is closing to help your customer take every relevant step along the way. Every sales process has a beginning, middle and end. It may have six steps or it may have fifty steps. In real estate, the business that I have been in for 25 years, it sometimes has hundreds of steps that have to be gone through to completion. The key is to understand the necessary steps in your industry, and to have a flowchart to guide you through your own process.

Buyers Buy

There is an old adage that asks, "How do you know you are working with a buyer? A buyer who buys, buys." That is the bottom line and it sounds pretty simplistic, but a buyer takes every relevant step along the way. For example, in real estate, if you ask them to make an appointment, they make an appointment and they show up on time. If you ask them to go look at property, they show up on time and they look at property with you. If you ask them to bring a checkbook so if they find a home they like they can make a deposit, they bring the checkbook. If you ask them to sign disclosures and documents appropriately to get the process started, they sign off on those documents. So a buyer who buys takes every relevant step along the way. When a buyer stops taking relevant steps is when you are probably running into indifference or objections. When you encounter indifference and objections, you need the skills to overcome them.

Indifference and objections are not bad things. It is often simply the negative side of a buying signal. Indifference occurs when they don't think they need your product. Remember if they were not objecting to things, then they wouldn't even be caring enough to spend the time and energy to debate you about it. They wouldn't be hesitant if they didn't have some level of interest. Sometimes objections are a drawback because it's something your product can't address, or the pricing and product don't match up. The objection could also be due to a misunderstanding. When people are not moving forward because they misunderstand something about your product, service or value, it is just a matter of cleaning that up through your process.

As you close, you are doing a summary and then you move onto your action step. What do you want them to do next? How do you take them through the process of summarizing where they are today, and then go on to the next relevant action step that takes them to the next process?

Business Systems

You obviously have systems which you've developed along the way. With any business you have to have very viable systems. These systems are vital. You have your administrative, operational, legal and technology systems. It is essential that those systems operate like clockwork. Every step must be broken down from A to B to C, all the way down to Z. Everything has its place and everything has its order. Everything needs to be as proficient as it possibly can be, with each step as important as the other, with no time wasted. If possible try to have only one single point of entry in communication within your infrastructure, whether it is data entry or in communication with your employees or with management. This is also true for technology and systems that speak to each other, including software programs, Internet programs, administrative programs, and other systems that help keep your business running. Getting as much information as you can from your customer and pushing it immediately out to all who need it and getting it into systems is key. People do not like double entry into systems or having to repeatedly answering the same questions along the way.

Consider how those systems can create an ideal experience for the consumer, so it's an easy process for them to go through. Make sure there is a check and balance all the way through. This may be redundant in some cases, but it underscores what they are getting, what they got or what they will receive. In addition, within your system make sure there is an easy way for them to fix any problem that may arise as they go through your process. Hopefully those problems are few and far between, but if there is a problem, have a system for it. Know what happens, know how quickly it happens, know who handles it, and make sure the person who handles it gets notified in a timely fashion. Having systems in place is truly, truly key.

Strategic Seduction

The sales process is really the art of strategic positive seduction. Although that sounds a little manipulative, buying something is an emotional purchase for many people. Most of the time we think of seduction in a sexual way, but this is not sexual by any means for this purpose. That said we all know sex sells and it is used directly or subtly in main marketing and ad campaigns. It clearly has its place. It is seduction to attract people to the product or service they say they want. This is about attracting and seducing them to something that you know that in your heart of hearts, if they take the time to review it with you, that it has value and that the consumer can benefit from it. Many times when people are buying not for a need or a necessity. Many times it is more about want and a purchase with discretionary income. Seduce them through all of their emotions, enticing their senses of smell and sight, how they hear, and view, while you also mirror their body language, if in person. The art of seduction is something that any good salesperson has to understand regarding what will work and what their messaging is. What is going to convey value proposition, and how will that work for each client and situation?

The Message

First think about what you want your potential customers to see. There are many underlying layers in terms of how you want them to see things. If you are doing an ad online or in print in a magazine, what image and colors do you want them to see? What feeling do you want people to experience? What are you trying to arouse in them emotionally that keeps them wanting more? What is the problem you are trying to solve for them? How do you meet or match them so they see there is a possibility of a solution? Maybe you have the answer, or your product has the answer, that can fulfill that special need for them. Then you want to show people why me, or why the product?

Understand how all this works together in your situation. Really take doing your homework seriously. When you have a potential client looking at or listening to your message (or both, in the case of video), they realize they have a problem, that there is a possibility it can be solved, and they realize that maybe you have a solution. They are either going to listen further on the phone, in person, or click on the next option on your website to go to the next section.

Next, what is your call to action? What do you want them to do? Buy my product, click here, do this, take the next step, fill out this form, get this free giveaway, whatever that might be. What do you want people to do next? You want to ask for their permission. Can you take them to the next level? This is key online and in person. As you take them through the next process, there is a real art about asking for permission from the consumer to offer them more value. You also want to ask their permission to get information from them that would help you through the process of taking them through this funnel. Sometimes this is subtle and sometimes direct and obvious.

Converting Your Mindset

There is the overall mindset, a worldview, which you have to keep in mind. How does the world view this product or service as a mass market? How would they view this consumer buying this product or service? Would the worldview look at them favorably? Is it something that they want to do hush, hush, and quiet behind the scenes? Or is it something that the consumer wants to do and have everybody know about? Also, what is the self-view? How does the self, the person who is buying, how do they feel about it? How do they see it? How do they experience it and do they care what everyone else thinks? Do they want others to see them in any particular way in relation to what they're buying from you? Understanding some of these key questions can be very helpful in guiding, helping and leading your customers.

Application of Your Message

Are the people and organizations you want to respond to your marketing message actually applying what you're asking them to do? This could be through applications, through questions that get checked off, or putting something on their Facebook page. It could be that you qualified them through that arena. Some people have free giveaways where their prospects have to fill out questions to get the offer. Some people have very extensive questions that take the prospect a much longer time to complete page after page after page. Some are very quick and easy to complete.

One of my friends and previous coaches has 40 questions on his survey. As you go through the questionnaire you realize that you are getting very intrigued by the questions. The questionnaire actually takes the person through a sequence that gives them an experience of feeling intrigued, edgy, and mixed with an expected intrigue. It either keeps the consumer engaged or they drop off. If they drop off and they don't finish the process, then you know this may not be a consumer or a client with an interest in your particular product. Then, two or three pre-qualification questions may be all you need.

I found this to be a very interesting way to discern consumers. Once you have asked for permission and you are converging their mindset into the proper worldview, self-view and path, you can determine whether or not there might be a fit. How do you get them to apply your process to keep being more qualified, especially if this is an online process? If it is in person, it is a little bit easier because you've got a visual of their body language and eye contact. You may be giving them a cup of coffee and you may be sitting in a conference room, so it might be easier to convince them to give you the necessary time to go through the qualifying process. If it is online or over the phone, you have at most seconds to attract and keep these people engaged.

Seller vs. Buyer

This step is about you. You take action to see if there is a yes or a no. Once you find out if there is a yes or a no, what do you do next? For everything that you get involved with, know that it's fine if there's a yes, and if there's not, that's fine too. But if there is a yes then you clearly want to get them engaged in the next step. What is their next step? It could be the next level of an appointment, getting a credit card, getting a check, signing a contract, or putting it in their online shopping cart and checking out online.

You also want to make sure that through the entire process you always have two call objectives. By the time you meet someone, call them, speak to them on the phone, or engage with them online, know that your first objective is to do Plan A. If Plan A doesn't work, then you always want to have Plan B in place. You want to go in prepared for your presentation. You want to be clear about your scripting, dialogue and your information, so that Plan A is the path that you are going down. Then boom, you run into some hurdles and objections. At that point you know immediately that it triggers your Plan B. Plan B would be a different script and approach, but every time you meet with a client or you engage them online or in person, know what your objective of Plan A or B would be. Then you are constantly prepared as a salesperson that is giving your client or consumer respect. You have maintained your integrity very well as a professional and as a salesperson, but also you are trying to do need/satisfaction selling. You are uncovering and satisfying their needs with your products' or services' features and benefits. Then see the connection for them and hopefully the clients are selling themselves and taking every relevant step. As a selling overview this is the strategic seduction of selling, and this is how it works.

Think of the power, if in addition to teaching yourself and your salespeople the strategic seduction of selling, you also teach your employees how to do this. When your employees understand how to use some of these skills as they communicate in their roles within the company, the sales skills can help keep people engaged, and help people to see your points of view, or to actually purchase whatever it is you are selling. Sometimes we are selling ideas. Sometimes we are selling a vision. Sometimes we are selling a dream. Sometimes we are selling a product.

Everyone is always selling something. My 5-year-old little granddaughter may be trying to sell Poppi on taking her to the park or to the zoo, to buy her something, or to get me to let her stay up late. It may be my wife selling me on why we need to do something, to take a trip or buy something. Or I'm persuading her about why we need to take a certain path or invest in something. The government is selling the idea of why people need to vote a certain way. There is always this art of selling, the art of seduction, the art of intrigue. This tapping into people's emotions is one of the most powerful things you can do. Sell from emotion and sell from passion. You also sell into people's future and what they will be, do or have once they commit. Don't sell in the present or past, but in the future.

Make sure you are still selling with complete integrity in any particular transaction for that particular client. Integrity is always the bottom line. There may be calculated steps, but you can still do them with truth and integrity.

Golden Nuggets

 Actually draw out the details of your sales process in a flow chart.

 Draw out how your business systems support your sales process.

 Know the steps you take your customer through, from initial contact to close.

 Know the follow up steps after the sale that keep your customer engaged with you.

 Remember: Integrity is always the bottom line.

Chapter **10**
Operations and Infrastructure

So far in this book I've been writing about the dream, sales, marketing, morale, and recruiting. These are all integral parts of building the revenue side of the business. But what is equally as important is having the proper infrastructure, systems and processes. It is important to make sure that your infrastructure is really well planned and thorough. This is one of those stages where it's important to look objectively at your own skills. If this is not one of your areas of expertise, find someone who can help you build the particular infrastructure that's needed.

If you're a smaller home-based business and you won't have any or many employees, it's very different than if you are planning on building into a larger company with infrastructure, bricks and mortar, and various departments. But even in a smaller operation there is still a need to have a process and an operations system in place.

Think about the administrative side of your business. This includes your financial, books, monthly P&L's, balance sheets - the whole financial piece. You also have your operational side, which takes care of running your business. Sometimes the finance person and the operation person are the same. This is often a dual role or sale, especially in the early days of being an entrepreneur.

The operational side can encompass anything from handling the employee aspect of the business to the supporting sales side. This person usually deals with the administrative and operational pieces to make sure that transactions and functions flow appropriately. They understand the technology, equipment needs, and facilities. They make sure that the people running those particular divisions understand how to get the best equipment, materials and tools that are needed at the lowest possible price in exchange for something that's going to be a fit for your business.

Flow Chart

Let's break this all down into a flow chart. Think about it this way for a moment. If you put a quarter in a machine and it finally comes out the bottom, then you're not getting your drink. Or if you put a quarter (and these days, many quarters) into the machine, you see it's going through the machine, then something starts spinning around, and finally then your drink pops out at the bottom. You have a successful working system. You can test the machine time and time again to make sure it works. It should work the same every time.

It is similar for each step that needs to happen in your own business to get the end result you want. Think through each step that needs to happen for your business to flow, and each transaction that needs to happen to meet your goals for the business.

Once you have a client, and your client has decided to put a quarter in the machine, they will want something in return. They expect either a product or a great experience, or a great experience along with that product. If someone is going to

219

walk into a Starbucks and throw down $4 or $5 for a latte, you want to make sure that when they're walking out the door, they've had the memorable experience so they don't think about spending the money for a cup of coffee somewhere else.

Your customer has an expectation as to what the operational side will be. They expect good service and a smooth experience. They want to use their iPhone in a transaction, get the appropriate receipt, have a coffee that's hot and in the right cup, and they have their cup sleeve. All of the steps they have to go through are the operational side of the business.

How does that process get created? Someone understands it completely. If you buy a McDonald's franchise, they have everything systematized and down to a science from the time the consumer pulls into a parking lot or drive-thru to the time they leave.

Let's say you're selling Internet products online through Amazon and you have a whole system and process you have to go through. You can be assured that Amazon and your distributors already have something in place. See now how you will be the added element in the process and map out your own operations to mirror a similar smart process behind the scenes. Obviously doing your due diligence on what already exists is best. Don't reinvent wheels if you don't have to. There are many options that already provide a toolbox of processes that you don't have to reinvent. Do your homework. Later, once you're up and running and generating cash flow continue to streamline and reinvent your process to make it even better.

If you're not a home-based business or an online business and you actually have bricks and mortar, with facilities and locations, then you have to get a little bit wider in your scope of what your operational piece can be so it can be reduplicated in other facilities.

Duplication

At the peak of running one of Prudential's companies, we had 105 offices in a territory that stretched from San Luis Obispo to San Diego, California. We had a very wide territory. Each of those offices had between 3,000 to 10,000 square feet in facilities, and anywhere from 30 to 150 people in each of the buildings.

It can be a very different business when you're running bricks and mortar business, and understanding operations that have many moving pieces such as phone systems, copy machines, equipment, computers and networks. The entire infrastructure is sometimes not as appealing these days, which is why many businesses are going virtual. Many businesses have found that by working with consumers online they're reducing cost and able to get better bottom line results.

But if you're in a retail business and you are selling products face to face with your customers, or you're a business that has bricks and mortar, you will have to figure out how to make that work. The key is to duplicate whatever systems you have so it's the same in every branch that you have.

Each office needs to be streamlined consistently in all branches, starting with the facilities when you walk into the receptionist, to the processes she uses to do her daily administrative work, to your operational administrative person who handles all the files and the documents for finance and related systems. You're really creating a unique system.

The key is to find ways to create or to develop the best systems for your particular business, or to use off the shelf systems that already exist. Sometimes people who have developed a great system replicate it in the franchising world. You clearly can find programs and systems online or for sale that you can plug, play and adapt.

Many times in the franchise business, whether you're buying a Subway, McDonald's, real estate or some other franchise, they have many of these systems in place. As a new franchise owner you'll get manuals and training in their step-by-step processes. They have recommendations as to cost for key items to be purchased. They have vendors you can choose that they've already vetted, and that have preferred pricing.

You may want to research your industry and see if a franchise or a joint venture type marketing consulting firm has put all of this in one place and may have what you need. My suggestion is before you go out and reinvent the wheel by building all of this yourself, do a lot of homework first.

Put the quarter in the machine from the top, let it go all the way to the bottom and figure out how it's going to flow, and how quickly and easily it flows. The way you're going to know that is if you're already in the business. If you're breaking away from a business and starting your own, then you already know what's been working in your previous company, and what didn't work so well for you.

Let's say you're breaking away from a corporate position. You already know how the systems work and you're now starting your own similar business. You probably have a pretty good roadmap as to what that needs to be in a smaller startup business.

Creating Your Process

Write everything down on a piece of paper, in an Excel spreadsheet, on a computer, or however you're going to do your homework. Write out every step that's needed from A, B, C, D, all the way to Z. And make sure you have thought out every process. Seek help where you need it.

Then go through your list. Is this something that's automated? Is it something that's done through technology once it's in? Or does it need a person to be involved in that particular option? Once you've detailed each step, you've mapped out a systematic flowchart of how your business flows from the first time the consumer engages with your company, employee or salesperson, to the time they close out their transaction. Their experience will be similar whether it's in a registration, in a legal document, or through online purchases.

Go through your list again and make sure everything that needs to happen is on your list. There may be forms to be filled out, monies to be exchanged, or different checkpoints that have to happen within the transaction. Maybe it's a one-time transaction and it's easy. Swipe a card, get the product, send through the mail and it's done.

Or maybe, as in the real estate business, there are numerous levels to process and evolve through. It can be a 30 to 60-

day process or longer in dealing with a consumer with many required steps to go through. Whether it's financing, title escrow, contracts, deposits, or inspections, you need your operations and systems mapped out and fine-tuned. In real estate, the entire process can be very cumbersome, so simplifying things as best you can for your customer is advised.

But you have to have a system. You need checklists and to think through the most streamlined process that works in your situation. And you also have to figure out how you can handle the least amount of data entries possible so you can have one point of data entry. You don't want to have to keep reduplicating your steps. Think about the process of people and employees handling these steps. How can you streamline their workflow so it's as smooth as possible? Think about what you can do to not create redundancies for either the consumer or employee. How can you give the consumer the best experience possible?

Again, the very first starting point for your homework is to draw the schematic and find out what steps are needed from A to Z to get your product to the consumer, distributed and closed out.

If you're not sure how all these things work, it is incredible what you can find online. Go to *Google* and search "Checklist for coffee shop," or "How do I set up a doggie wash facility?"

If you want to set up a real estate office, you can go online and type in "All different types of real estate franchises." You will be amazed on what you can find on people's websites that are sample lists of how to do X, Y and Z or on blogs.

A lot of this work is more about homework than it is about reinventing the wheel. What I have found about being an entrepreneur is if you have a unique idea, that's great. That's where your goal can be. Most of the systems and processes for setting up a business have been done hundreds of thousands of times before. So take advantage of what's been done in the past and do your homework. Borrow legally where you can, and invest or invent the rest.

It will save you a lot of money, because in the infrastructure you have to think about details. The many details about the administrative process and the operational side of running a business to make sure that the operation is flowing, will become clearer as you write them down. Make sure there is consistency in product development, in the service, and in checks and balances in your products being delivered. From the production and operations side, make sure that the assembly line of your product or service is flowing.

The administrative side is typically about the finance and technical paperwork or online processes that need to happen to make sure that your business is compliant. The processes ensure that it's financially sound and savvy, and that you're saving as much on the administration of running a business as possible while having your books balance. The operational piece will ensure the infrastructure is actually working and running. Both should dovetail hand in hand.

Your salespeople are responsible for funneling everything into the assembly line. First of all, they need to get it on the conveyor belt. The people working on the operational side of the company keep that whole assembly line working. If you think of a conveyor belt going down along a runway with various machines, it has to go through, at each step stamping something, packaging something or folding something—that is the operational side of any business.

So just think about it. Does one person do everything in a particular step, or is the task shared? As an entrepreneur, are you going to do all of those jobs for the first six months? Are you going to be the salesperson, administrative person, operations person and the legal person? That's often how entrepreneurs start.

But if you can hire or outsource as you grow, that's when you want to find your talent who can do that work for you, or who knows it better than you know it.

Picture What You Want

It's important to clearly understand what you want and who you want. What are you looking for? Usually it's much better, when you're trying to build a house, to visit the architect with sketches to illustrate what you already have in mind. You may have pulled pictures out of magazines or online, or maybe you've taken pictures of other houses. This makes it easy for you to give the architect an idea of what you're looking for. It really helps to create and fine-tune what you're building for yourself.

As you're building your company, think about this as well. It would be like you're building a house and you've been collecting ideas and information for quite some time. And in this case you're going to your operational team, your

226

administrative team, and your tech team to create and sketch out the plans.

Building Your Tech Team

Often times, the tech team consists of two different types of people. The tech person is involved in the backend systems of technology, making sure your printers, computers, and networks are all running smoothly. This is actually one of many positions that can be outsourced to save money.

You can outsource tasks that involve simply a consultation with them, or when you only need someone a few hours a month or a week. Absolutely outsource where you can, until you have a need for an employee to handle that task full time internally. It saves you a lot of money in time, payroll, insurances and in taxes. I highly recommend that when you can outsource things, absolutely do so.

In the particular company I was running, we did have a tech person who handled computer hardware and printers for all of the offices. For us, technology was a central part of our infrastructure, and it was a full time job.

In addition to the technical person running your equipment, you also have technology and marketing people who are turning the dials on the Internet marketing world with social media, websites, and online presence. That's a whole other type of techie. Both pieces are vital to any business being successful. If you have the luxury of hiring someone internally who can work with you daily in your business creation, do so. It can ramp up your business swiftly. But this is also something you can outsource. Do your homework and test them out on a few smaller projects to start.

As you think about outsourcing in your particular situation, understand the components you need within your own toolbox to run your business.

Homework is Key

I can't emphasize enough how important it is to spend time doing homework. Once you have your idea and you're passionate about it, it's very easy to get excited about how your logo will look, how your marketing will look, how your storefront will look, how your website will look, and how your business cards will look. That's the fun piece of it.

But it's sometimes more difficult to make sure that the operational, administrative, and legal sides of your company are equally as sound, because that really is the foundation that everything else is built upon. I really encourage you to spend the research and time to make sure that everything is working from the get-go within your organization.

On the legal side, there are many services you can pull in for an extra amount of hours or just as you need them on a project. Many times the legal cost during the startup phase of a company is much higher than it is during the maintenance phase each month. Get references and referrals and compare hourly rates. Ask what services they may offer on a project flat fee basis and agree on all that up front and in writing. Make sure they know when and how you want to be communicated with on billing approval and hours.

Find an attorney you trust and respect. You might find your attorney through a referral, or you can look online. You can interview some people via phone or through your business or affiliate network. But an attorney should be outsourced versus in-house initially. You don't need an ongoing attorney full time.

There are also various sites and services like Legal Shield which I have recently joined and became a member of to help me have easy access and streamline my cost. These really help small business excel quickly and get to the right people to help you early in the process. When you're setting up businesses in terms of getting incorporated, are you going to be an LLC, S Corp or C Corp? They all have their own benefits, pros and cons. I'm not here to give you any kind of legal advice. I'm not a legal person or a finance or tax person. But I am here to say that services exist out there that can dramatically streamline the aspect of starting a business if you take time to do your research online.

In the long run it can save you thousands, if not millions of dollars, if you legally protect yourself in contracts that are being signed, leases that are being signed, and employment contracts. So make sure you get the absolute best legal advice when you're setting up any infrastructure for legal partnerships or your company in general. When you're setting up your infrastructure, make sure you're getting absolutely phenomenal tax advice as to the best corporate structure to set up for your business, and your best tax consequences for what you're trying to accomplish.

In terms of the legal structure of your corporation, you might start out as one entity such as an LLC and you eventually transition into a sub S corporation or a C corporation. But if you do your homework you'll know at which stage which legal structure makes financial sense. Get the right advice from tax people to help you make the right choices.

If you're doing X amount of revenue, X amount of transactions with X amount of employees and you're selling in one city, what type of structure works best for you that's going to get you the best economic return on taxes, legal structure and your legal rights? And what's going to be most cost-effective?

This would be versus a business that you're looking to scale, one that's going to be nationwide, either online or with bricks and mortar. Is it going to have many employees and salespeople? Is it a high litigious type business like real estate? You might have a completely different structure within that type of operation, because you know what you're scaling to, versus a small home based business.

Avoid Costly Oversights

The Department of Real Estate, which became the Bureau of Real Estate in the real estate space, changed from DRE to BRE just about two years ago. They only allow certain entities and structures to have a license registered with a state, which for me was California. Make sure you have structures and systems in place that keep you updated on important changes in your industry.

Remember to do all of your homework online and also ask your attorney if there are any regulations that will restrict you from doing what you want, whether it's federal or local or state regulation. What regulations must you adhere to?

If you do your homework you're less likely to go down a path that you're really excited about, and then all of a sudden you find out you needed to have a handler's permit or a certain corporate structure. And that it takes six months to get it approved and you thought you were opening next week. Or you thought that you didn't have to have your salespeople licensed and certified under a certain governmental agency and you then find out that you do.

I cannot stress enough to slow down on launching your business until you've taken the time to do your homework, getting your business all set up and ready to go. The way that makes the most sense to me is to write it out on paper, vet it with those who you know can give you the right advice in those sections, and then test it.

Dry Run Exercises

Do a dry run through your systems before you launch to the open public, making sure you're putting the quarter into the machine and letting it go all the way through. Repeat the experience to make sure it works each time. Fix any redundancies or missing steps. Clarify instructions for the people who will be using the system. Find out where your bugs might be. Ask your technician and your administrative people what would work and what wouldn't at various volumes of business and be ready to adjust along the way.

I also recommend, after you get it all in place, to do a dry run if you can have everybody in one meeting or on a conference call. These might be people that you're interviewing, or they may be people that you're setting up as advisers and consultants in your business.

Have them all in one room or in one Skype session and have them run through the entire roll-out of how the company is going to work and how the infrastructure is going to be set. Do it almost as if you are pitching this company and the whole thing to a group of investors, explaining what worked and how your visions are going to grow. Be clear about how they're going to make a return on their money.

What's different in this particular meeting I'm suggesting is that you actually open up the curtain and show them the infrastructure from beginning to end. It will be a very detailed and cumbersome meeting, but it's a very valuable thing to have so that the legal department can hear what the marketing tech people are thinking about doing and that the operations people can hear that the computer guy wants to do XYZ.

It is amazing to have all of this collective consciousness on one call or in a conference room. Sometimes the experience puts up roadblocks, or detour signs, yellow lights or red lights about something you thought was going to work perfectly. And it absolutely won't because the technology system is not available or the legal guys say you can't legally do that. Make sure before you spend all of your money to get your business open, or you launch your website, that you're really ready to run. Make sure that you've thought all of these things out. This could be just you if you are a solopreneur, but you can get advice and use people as sounding boards along the way.

Franchise Options

If you're buying a franchise, many systems have been created for you. There are major pros and cons to that as well. Obviously you have the cost of a franchise. You have the setup aspect and many legal things to go through. Often there are down payments. You're limited within their systems. You may have to use their name. There are tradeoffs just like anywhere else in life.

Marriage is wonderful and great. I've been married 25 years, but there are tradeoffs of being married versus being single. And when you have a partnership in business, there are tradeoffs of being in a partnership versus being an individual who makes all the decisions.

It's great to have a partner to bounce ideas off and to carry the ball when you're tired, and to have synergy and energy to brainstorm. But if for some reason the partnership starts going astray, it can be very ugly to be in a partnership that you are miserable in, and that is just bringing down the business and not working. Make sure you're always realizing and exploring both ends of the coin. Remember there's no perfect world, there's no perfect business and there's no perfect relationship. But find out which you think is going to work best for you by writing things out, talking things out with others and getting advice.

I have had many great experiences over the years with the franchise side of the business. And ultimately for me, I had negative experiences. I got locked into a franchise that sold me something that originally was aligned with my dream and vision. But it was sold a year and a half after I bought into it. The parent company that bought it had a whole different direction and vision for their future path. That all had a dramatically negative impact on my business. We ended up becoming the redheaded stepchild in the franchise system of the various companies they owned.

It did end up harming my business. Even though I had a case legally get out of this franchise, it did not come to pass because I was legally bound to a longer period of time in the franchise agreement. Without spending an exorbitant amount on legal fees and fighting in court, I couldn't get out of bed with them.

So, it ended up restricting what I could do within that company in terms of growth, territory, bringing in partners, new equity opportunities and ultimately for a sale. It ended up being something that was not of benefit to me at all at the very end.

In my first go-around with the franchising world, I had a very good experience. My second was not so good. I think that such is life. For you, if you find opportunities that you want to pursue, I highly recommend getting advice up front on the pros and cons of both. Then Accept that there is no way to foresee every circumstance and possibility.

But the bottom line of all this is to make sure that you don't spend more time on your marketing, sales and promotions, and neglect the high importance of operations, administration, technology and legal. It will be crucial to meld those altogether so that your company is balanced and integrated in a very strong way.

Ultimately everything goes back to customer perception and creating a phenomenal experience for them. How do your customers see this as seamless? How do they have a phenomenal interaction with you so that you can create raving fans from the beginning of your funnel when you're attracting the client, to the very end of that connection once they've had the sale and they've walked out the door? How will they feel about their interaction with you and your company when they're walking out with something in their hand, or they've finished the experience that you provided for them? How do you create raving fans for the future so you have a client for life? That's really the key.

Golden Nuggets

 Create a flowchart that shows every aspect of your operation and how things get done.

 Create processes that can easily be duplicated in new offices, to ensure consistency across your organization.

 To avoid having to reinvent the wheel, look online to find processes developed by others in your field.

 Build your administrative and tech team as needed, as your enterprise grows.

 Consult an attorney early in your planning stages, to avoid future delays and costs.

 Do a dry-run exercise to test your system before putting it into production.

Chapter **11**
Your Customers: Life or Death

No matter what business you're in, the importance of the customer is key to not only developing and creating your product from the beginning, but also in attracting the customer or the client. I interchange those words, *customer* and *client.* I'll talk about why I see the difference between the word *customer* and *client,* and how I differentiate that in my thinking.

When entrepreneurs have their dream in mind about what they want to create, it's usually for someone else. It's an expression of themselves in the world. They would like to make a mark or make a difference for other people, or in a larger arena, the world. Sometimes the ideas, vision, products or services are grandiose and worthy enough that some people really do have a vision that will help change the world.

Look at groups like Google, Facebook and Netflix or charitable organizations like Make a Wish Foundation or Ronald McDonald House that have really helped change the world. These organizations all started with an idea or a vision. Somebody just wanted to make a difference. Someone thought this would have value and they should be the one to deliver it.

Turning Lack into Advantage

When I see products and services evolve, it's originated either from someone who thinks they can do it better, more effectively, more cost effectively, faster with more flair, creating more of an experience, doing it with new panache or doing it for a current or new generation. Usually when I see those things becoming a reality, it's because an individual or an organization has been lacking that experience in the marketplace.

There is a local cabinet company in San Diego that does commercials on television. They talk about how when they are putting cabinets and shelving in their homes that they were just not getting the services and products that they desired, so they decided there had to be a better way. Because of their experience they went on to create a very, very successful cabinetry and shelving company that is one of the top in San Diego. Through their own frustration with the marketplace, they identified something lacking, and from their experience they decided they could do it better.

In my process of hiring real estate agents over the last 25 years I would ask applicants why they got into real estate. Most people would say it's because they wanted to help someone, they wanted to make a difference, they enjoyed seeing houses or they wanted to make a lot of money.

Other people said sometimes it was because they had a really bad experience with a realtor when their families were buying or selling homes. Sometimes it was a very traumatic experience. Perhaps the husband was being relocated or the family was deciding to move from one town to another, or maybe the family was outgrowing its home because they just had more children and were expanding their family. It was really sad to hear that they had a bad experience moving in and out of homes, which should have been one of the most joyous experiences they ever had in helping people build a better life.

Moving Cross-Country

I remember hearing one story from a family who was moving from Michigan to California. They'd had a long, long escrow. They had fallen out a couple of times as they were doing this long distance. There was a lack of communication with the real estate agent and unfortunately, also with the lender.

In that process, they finally got a house after getting into escrow on another property the second or third time. It was for a home that they really, really wanted. And they had many, many complaints along the way with late paperwork, late emails coming through, additional documentation that was needed by the real estate agent who asked two or three times for the same information they knew they had already sent. Along with all of this was additional cost throughout the transaction that they weren't expecting.

As this process continued, they felt increasingly frustrated. It's stressful enough to move. Any of us know what it's like to move your family from one home to another, let alone from one city or state to another. And these people more than had their hands full with three small children under the age of six, with both parents working.

This is a very typical household today in the United States. What should have been a very joyous experience for them became a burden, full of doubt, fear and anxiety. They had put their Michigan home on the market and it had sold. They had to be out of their house and that transaction was going very smoothly. They knew that they were under a time crunch and a huge pressure to get the California transactions completed.

The husband, who was relocating because of his job, had a certain time he had to be in San Diego to start his job. His wife was going get the family situated and look for work after they settled in. The difficulties they had along the way during their real estate purchase in California created undue stress on their family.

I heard about this unfortunate situation at the tail end of the transaction. At the time I was the President of the company in which I was working. I wasn't the owner or the CEO at that time. This goes back quite a few years.

I got a call the day they were supposed to close. The call was clearly from an irate customer, which is how I met these people. Rightfully they had screamed and yelled at the real estate agent who was not able to get anything done to help them during the process.

As they revealed their story to me, I learned that their moving truck was arriving and they were supposed to be moving in that particular day. They were supposed to have reported documentations and loan documents and closed their escrow the day before so they would be able to move in that following morning. They called me that following morning, the day they expected to move into their new home.

Unfortunately, it looked like escrow was not going to close as scheduled, and that they were going to be sitting on the street with their moving truck and all of their belongings. At the very last minute the lender had requested required documents that everyone seemed to have forgotten about. Even though the buyers thought they had gotten in all of the papers, the lender didn't agree.

This particular experience became a nightmare because the property ended up getting delayed another two days. The family had to stay in a hotel. The moving van incurred additional charges because they had to store it for a few extra days. It created a lot of ill will, discomfort, and anger within this particular family.

Long story short, a year or so later when I was teaching one of my classes, and who was in the class but this particular client. On that fateful day a year earlier they had called me as the head of the company and said, "What can you do about this?" I had gotten on the phone with lenders and title reps and tried to facilitate getting things done. I think I saved a little time, but there wasn't anything I could do to save the day at the end of the very last 11th hour.

But this experience caused this particular woman to go into the real estate business and she ended up getting a real estate license. I met her in one of the classes. We did handle it better at the end of the transaction. In time we did save some aggravation for them, and we gave her some closing gifts and some additional credits for her home.

We ended up trying to make the very, very best of a bad experience. We did a lot of follow up afterwards. I got another real estate agent involved. We made sure that their

241

home warranty was taken care of. We tried to create a raving fan out of a really nightmarish situation.

It was a little too late, a day short, but this particular woman had a lot of opportunities to go work for various companies. She chose to come and work with my company, Prudential Real Estate. She realized Prudential had a very good name and she wasn't going to base her entire perspective of how she saw the real estate industry on one agent. She didn't allow this experience to diminish the brand of the company. The brand had value to her and she also liked how I had handled and dealt with the situation. She appreciated the customer service once I got involved, which caused her to end up joining us as a real estate agent within our company.

Her desire was to make sure, as she started her new career in San Diego, that it was going to be a learning experience for her. She wanted to make sure that she could smooth the process for any of the customers that she worked with. In addition, she would learn to do it better and bigger, more concrete, more concise and more thorough than anybody else she had ever worked with. She also thought it would be a great way to earn a lucrative income for herself and her family. She went on to be a very, very successful real estate agent.

Marketplace Transparency

I shared that story because many times people who have bad experiences can go on to be your worst nightmare. With *Yelp* and customer online reviews people can voice their opinions, desires, dissatisfactions, expectations and their experience of delivery of your product or service. Within moments of working with you they can provide a scathing review online or give very high praises regarding how they felt about a company. This is a very transparent world with a very loud, strong voice from the consumers who are now empowered more than ever before to let the industry, the community and marketplace know how transparent the customer service is or is not with an organization.

It helps raise the game on a lot of us, and a lot of people in any industry. It creates the responsibility that should have always been there, that the customer is always right and the customer needs to be served. Personally I don't necessarily believe that the customer is always right, but I believe that how you approach and deal with them can make them feel like they're right even if they're wrong, to help solve the situation.

This plays right into the concept of turning '*Lead to gold*'. In this case it worked out as a benefit for both. This woman found a new career and our firm got a great new productive, committed agent.

Game Changers

A person who creates products or services has the end in mind, both in terms of results and the customer's experience. "What can I do better? What can I do more efficiently? And how do I create that?" So many great products have been created. Look around at the things we have available today—with Apple and Samsung devices and the whole mobile device industry, and how that's changed and evolved over the years.

The movie industry has dramatically changed as well. Even though there are still movie theaters, many times they're half full or close to empty. In Cinepolis Luxury Theaters where I live, you sit in a lounge, laidback chair and have waiters wait on you. It's a high-end ticket item versus the regular movie theaters. Another example of a '*Lead to gold*' experience is people want to be able to watch streaming movies on television. Netflix completely changed the game in the industry for movies and for people who like to watch movies and shows. Think about how the consumer's desire changed an industry and inspired products and services that fit them better. There is a market where people are willing to pay for what they want and need if it's of value or better.

Look at what Uber has done to the taxicab industry, and what Charles Schwab has done with their eSchwab product. It changed the stock brokerage business when they went to online trades at flat fees or reduced cost. The consumer began to realize that they could gain a lot of knowledge online, or maybe they already had the expertise themselves. This game-changing product gave them the ability to have less involvement with a broker. They were able to avoid paying for advice and direction while they enjoyed more of a wholesale pricing structure.

These kinds of business models are key. All you have to do is look at all the Costco stores that have opened up over the years where consumers are able to buy in bulk. They may not want to go to a grocery store and pay what they might consider high prices when they purchase items in bulk like paper towels, cups or large portions of food. They can go to the warehouse and get a better deal. People are lined up with huge carts to go through a wholesale warehouse type environment. They're not looking for the aesthetics. They're looking for the price, value and good deals.

When the Customer is Not Right

It is amazing what the marketplace can bear when someone has a need. Asking, "What can be filled?" is often how customers get served. The old adage says, "The customer is always right." I have found in real estate that the customer is not always right. Sometimes the customer is just downright wrong. However, it's the art and the finesse as to how you handle them, how you keep them calm, how you listen to their concerns, how you repeat back to them what you heard them say that helps resolve the situation. The more upset they get, the calmer you have to stay.

Your calm, soothing voice is how you can help them understand that you are compassionate and empathetic, you are knowledgeable regarding what they're telling you, you are taking it seriously, and you realize it's a big issue for them. Once they're calm enough to hear you, you can start explaining to them how you can help them and how you can't. You can suggest who might be able to help them with the things you cannot help them with. It's all about letting people be heard and showing you care.

Sometimes customer service is not all about fixing the problem, even though that's the reason people state when they're complaining. It's really because they want to be heard. They feel disillusioned in what they were promised versus what they got.

Fewer Customer Complaints

How do you get fewer customer complaints in the first place? This is usually by being very, very thorough about what you offer in your products and services upfront.

245

Describe your step-by-step process clearly. Be very transparent about what they can expect, what they get, and what they don't get.

Sometimes they think they're paying for things that are really not intended. Somehow it's not a clear description of the service offering, or the fine print is so small that they aren't realizing that they didn't get that. Underscoring all of this up front is key.

Next make sure that communication happens every step along the way. Tell them what you're going to tell them. Tell them what you told them. Tell them again. And then follow up. This can be done through a series of phone calls, emails, surveys, conversations with real people, live, over the phone, Skype, and having a process in place that measures things all along the way.

Over-communication is really the key to always making sure you're connecting with your customer. The more opportunities you have to connect with them early in the process, throughout the process and then before the transaction is completed, is really the way in which you can keep customer service at its very, very height.

Timeline and Funnel

Another great tool is to draw out a customer timeline and a funnel. Create a diagram for everybody in the company so they understand from the very first contact with the client where they fit in. Whether the contact is online, in-person, on the phone, if they walk into a store, or if they're introduced with a handshake at a luncheon, everyone knows how to respond to that customer, or potential customer.

Everyone knows the company's step-by-step, A-B-C-D-E-F-G all the way through processes with an ideal customer and consumer experience.

How does that process look? Depending on the product or service they're buying (and you may have various products and services), how does that step-by-step process look? What would you have to do to create a *wow* factor?

The Wow Factor

A wow factor is where someone is just blown away, above and beyond, getting more than they expect with a great feeling, a great vibe. I refer to it sometimes as, "What can you do to create the mint on the pillow, the chocolate dipped strawberry experience?" Perhaps you've gone to hotels before where you might walk in the room and there are chocolate dipped strawberries. Or at night, your bed is turned down for you and it has chocolate mints on the little dish by your bed.

You think, "Oh, that was nice." It wasn't necessary. They didn't have to do it. They didn't have to provide that experience. But it was a tiny little extra touch that changed a feeling, a vibration or a thought that you had about the person who put it there, or the company itself.

So what can you do in your businesses with your customer experience to create that mint on the pillow or the chocolate dipped strawberry experience? I believe the way you do that is to understand the funnel and the diagram, and the timeline of your clients. Go back to the diagram you made of all of your company processes. Think of that quarter going into your machine, and how you've smoothed out every process. Now think of how you can add wow factors throughout the process for your customers. I recommend that whether you're an existing business, a startup business or in the middle stages of trying to grow, that you are constantly mapping out the customer experience.

Customer Communication

If you don't know fully what that is, map it out as best you can and then test what you have so far. Every month and every quarter, test again through checking out your customer surveys. I recommend having a customer survey process, both verbally and in print, that you send them along the way where you can ask for feedback about how are things are going. You can send them a "Thank you" for using your product or service, and include the supervisor's name in the e-mail, letter or phone call that says, "If you have any problems or issues beyond your normal contact person, here's how you can reach me."

You can also up sell by adding a message "Did you know that these things can also be done for you within our company?" If they are a happy customer, they may want to bring additional business to you, so give them additional steps and processes that can be done to help create these products and services. It will be a good experience for them.

When your customer has completed their transaction with you, have an immediate follow up. With the Uber experience, you never give them a credit card because it's already registered online. You are able to track that driver's progress towards reaching you from the very time you make the connection on your mobile phone to the time that they get to you. As soon as you step out of the car, you have an electronic receipt of what you paid. And it sends you an electronic survey so it's very easy to click a few stars if you thought it was a five-star experience or a one-star one.

Automation is important in any business. It makes the experience more enjoyable and the consumer realizes you do care, especially then when you do something about what they said. As you gain this feedback about how to better serve the consumer or the client and you start making those changes and additions, it's another great thing to promote.

Put it in newsletters. Put it in blog posts. Put it in Facebook posts. Put it in new offerings to your consumer. Put it into your e-mail database when you're sending out updates about your product and service offerings with messages like "We listen. We care what you say. Thank you for helping make our company better."

"Look what we've done because you spoke up." List some of the things you've done within your process not only for a particular consumer or client, but for all customers and consumers that are coming in, so that they can see what you constantly do to transition, transform and evolve into your highest good within your company, and within your employee process. Keep turning "Lead into Gold" and transition, transform to your highest good in your operations.

Customer service experience is not rocket science, but it's really hard to implement effectively. It's easy to understand and yet hard to do. But if you really nail this down, you can create a great customer experience. Realize that customers are the bloodline, breath, lungs and the oxygen of your company. As your body needs to survive and grow, so does your company. The breath in which you breathe the air—is really the customer. The cleaner and consistent air you have to breathe, the better your company will continue to flow and ebb in a really great process of growth and good will.

Alignment to the Core

If you can go back to your core values, whether you call it a mission statement, vision statement or a manifesto, let all of the decisions you make for your customers and consumers refer back to the core values of your company. Constantly be checking what you're doing in practice in relationship with what you say is important.

When you're in board meetings, team meetings, sales meetings or you're just meeting with yourself, think about what you're going to do next. Ask yourself whether this new addition, this new deletion, this new change or this new modification stays within the alignment of serving the customer at the highest-level possible. And does it stay in line with the other core values that you started and built your company around?

If you're constantly coming back to the decision-making process within what you're trying to stay pure and true to, you will find that you stay much more in integrity within your own self and your own company. And you will also continually evolve to provide a better company and customer experience.

Customer and Client

I differentiate between customer and client. I see a client as one you have a longer exchange of service with. I look at everyone as a customer because everyone is an acquisition opportunity to put products and services together with the consumer need, which becomes a customer. But the client is someone who you have an exchange of advice, direction and a longer engagement with. You might have repetitive transactions with a client that lead to more and more products and services from your service offering. A consumer is a possible relationship with one of these two categories you have yet to create.

As an example, some of my real estate agents had clients that bought two to six houses from them. In many cases they became friends, and friends of the family. Clients can also be defined as someone you have a legal fiduciary relationship with, such as an attorney or financial advisor.

A customer typically is someone who's buying a product. They might buy a computer, groceries, and a new pair of tennis shoes where a product is purchased which is usually a fairly quick exchange of that product or service.

I know these are interchangeable, but that's how I think about a client. A client is service-oriented in typically longer timelines. A customer is usually product-oriented. Specifically, this could be a customer who is buying from Amazon or another online retailer.

This doesn't mean that those customers don't deserve the same experience as clients. It might be a short five-minute experience of having to click, click, click online, but maybe

251

they're getting visual impact from your websites. There might be a quick 30-second video explaining the product that is enjoyable. Easy check-out could be a selling point, or perhaps there's a quick customer survey at the end and follow up emails to make sure they got their product in a timely fashion, and that they are happy with it.

Amazon does a phenomenal job of understanding these processes. Though it's sometimes annoying to people I know, they do a great job of upselling to other products. "Oh, you bought this. You might like this," or "So and so bought this, you might like this." For many people that becomes an annoyance, but this is a consumer-driven society and our consumerism in United States, individually, is at an all-time high. I don't think that's going away. And if you're in any business to sell products and services and to engage your customer, it's worth getting that communication out to them and letting them know they can engage in other ways with you. Sometimes you may offer them great deals and special purchases when you're trying to clear out your warehouse or offer promotions. Give them another chance and see if they'd like to engage or not.

Customer Control

Make sure that in your communication you're giving people the control to gauge how you communicate with them. This is why many sites that make it so easy, whether people want to have a monthly update or a weekly update every time there's a product, use text messaging or phone calls. Giving those options in your communication with your consumer experience at least makes the customer feel like they have choices and they won't just completely shut you off and click you out.

If your experience is too hard to maneuver through, it becomes an annoyance and there's no way for them to feel like they're in control. As a result, many times people just turn off and say, "Forget it" and they go on to the next part of the service even if you're trying to be helpful and to be of value. So make sure that at the top of your list is the ease of consumer experience. Make sure your customers are happy with the process. Know how it feels to them and what they're going through. Know that your products and services are delivered quickly, in a timely manner, efficiently and that they exceed expectations. Make sure that there is a fair price for what it is you're exchanging.

And if it's a high-end luxury item where there are many discussions, then you especially have to create the wow-experience through either your branding or marketing. Be aware of what they're achieving with you that makes them feel differently than what they can get from the masses. Know why they'd be willing to pay more for your product.

Many people want to pay for high-ticket items as long as they feel that they're in the elite. If you can make people elite, and that there's an exclusive small group that gets this and they're part of that group, people will pay. They'll become part of clubs, VIP groups or pay higher ticket dollar items to drive the car with a certain emblem on it. They will pay to be part of an elite executive club at the airport. Keep in mind this market also exists. You just have to realize what it is you're trying to communicate and get across in creating that experience.

At the end of the day, make sure that of all the things you do within your business, the customer is at forefront of your mind. Make sure you don't lose sight of that. Constantly do anything you can to improve the experience with them and for them.

Golden Nuggets

 When you have a frustrating experience as a customer, think about how you would solve that problem in your own business.

 Listen to customers who have problems with your company, and update your systems to avoid similar problems in the future.

 Learn how to deal graciously with disgruntled customers who may not be right.

 Be very thorough and explicit when describing up front what your customer can expect from you.

 Create a wow factor, and stay in communication with your customers.

 Remember your core values, and let all decisions reflect them.

Chapter **12**

Higher Power Google Earth

You've created your mission statement, you've diagrammed out all of your processes, and made sure each process aligns with your mission statement. You're the leader of this marvelous enterprise. What does that mean now? How can you be an effective leader?

For me, leadership doesn't just mean leading companies or leading people. For me, leadership means leading ourselves, meaning leading our own being. We all are made up of the many things that's needed and driving our lives. At each stage of our lives we are still all mentally, emotionally, physically, and spiritually connected as human beings as a whole. Remember our MEPS state assessment. We need to be aware of this every day and in every interaction with another.

And I believe that we all, if we're conscious and aware, have to learn to lead that being which is in ourselves. You are the conductor and the orchestra within your own stadium of your life, which can be small or large. Personally I've always had the desire to have a really large stage or a stadium or a global platform where I believe that there are no limits. Some people have different desires. Some people want to just focus on their family, children, career, or on their health. That really is enough for them and they have no desire to have higher purpose or a higher calling. They don't have the desire to make a difference in the world and I understand that. But making a difference in your own life to materialize those things is still important to being a happy, healthy, joyful, complete human being. That is as important as it is trying to radiate it out for others and be an example of who you are, or to lead others to that path.

Tapping into Power

I believe that as we're living our lives, running our business, and we're enjoying our favorite activities, that there is a deeper expression of joy through all that if we seek it. I think any time you can express creativity and joy you are expressing, and pulling down and through part of Higher Power and higher purpose. I enjoy helping people find and tap into that Higher Power, higher purpose or whatever they call it. Some call this nature, family, God, Jesus, whatever the phrase might be that it's named for them. I believe that, more often than not, finding and tapping into that presence helps fuel dreams to become a reality faster. Any time you are tapping into your genius or you are tapping into unknown sources, you are also tapping into the unknown mixed with what you do know, and that can be a very powerful combination.

There are ways to tap into this even further, and I believe that those ways are through writing, creating goals, journaling, masterminds and through meditation. The power and presence of meditation is very significant. This is particularly true in business, when you are realizing, "Okay, I'm trying to create a profitable business. I'm trying to create a business that I love. I'm trying to make a difference;" it's quite thrilling! Then you start to ask yourself, "What is at this smaller stage now, and what could it be at a bigger stage?" When you open up your mind to consciousness, of thinking what that can be at a much higher level, you sometimes can tap into ideas at your core you didn't know were there. This awareness can influence anything from the level where you start your business, your business offering, the way your company looks, your logos, colors, marketing, and ultimately the entire character of your business and its contribution to the world.

Another Perspective

I like to use an analogy. We've all seen the *Google* Earth app, where the little icon starts out either over a house or an address, and if you expand the *Google* Maps out, way out to the universe, you really get a huge bird's eye view, and then a satellite view of how this world or universe can look. I like thinking about that concept every time I think about doing something or making a change in my life related to my life or business. That's what I did on my previous path when I made a transition from my past business.

Think about that analogy. If you're sitting at your computer and you're looking at a house or a backyard where you can see the details on a *Google* Earth and you expand it out a little bit, you see the streets. You then expand out more, and you see the further neighborhood. When you scan it up higher you can see highways. Scan it up further you can see the cities, regions, and then other states. And you keep bringing it up, bringing it up, higher, higher, higher, bringing it up, you start seeing the United States. Then, you start seeing the rounding of the Earth and you see the blues and the greens and the different colors that are webbed in through all of that, and the flow of what looks like a beautiful child's painting that has a massive form around it.

Then you scroll up and scan further, and you start getting a global perspective of the world. You start pulling in stars and you're seeing the darkness of the sky with the reflection of the Earth shining back up to you.

Sit with that for a moment and realize how you feel differently if you're looking at that view, whether it's through *Google* Earth or just through your imagination. It's similar to standing on top of a roof looking out and you have a fairly good view of expansive horizons. You have a mix of feelings about what you're seeing. You have emotions and thoughts around this new view and perspective. Realize how differently you would feel, and you do feel, as you visualize and go up to that outer space level and you're sitting on a satellite. You have an astronaut suit on, and in that highest-tech astronaut outfit, you can comfortably get around.

You have some sort of jet pack so you can go wherever you want, but you're sitting up on a satellite just kicking a little bit of time, you know, having a cup of space latte. And as you look down on the Earth and at the planets around you, imagine how you would feel differently. Just get with these gut feelings. What are you feeling? What are you thinking? What are you thinking about in terms of possibilities? How small does the Earth feel compared to when you were on the roof? And if you were on the roof versus when you were on the satellite, what could you contemplate in your imagination and in the possibilities? What might be different?

Let's say you're looking at a house with other houses all around it in a neighborhood. You have some different thoughts about what you could do to create something within your own backyard, or with your neighbors if you're thinking of building something. Perhaps within that neighborhood you're thinking about creating a business, or within that, a new invention. You're thinking about what you could be creating. And there's still so many possibilities, thoughts, so many things you know you could do better than a current business does it now. There are things you know you could do differently or cheaper, better, or faster than any other business that you know. Or maybe you're creating a whole new business model that doesn't exist, or a new product.

These are all great imaginations to have within that view and within that framework. But think about that same mentality and imagination power, sitting way above on a satellite, sipping your space latte and then thinking about what is even more possible. Then get the last bird's eye view, when you can't actually see the houses, streets or the neighborhood, the states, the world. All you see is vast color and space. You then get a new higher, wider and more vast view that allows you new perspective and intuition.

The Joy Factor

I have used the *Google* Earth app every day of my life in theory. I check in with myself on my internal joy factor, I look at the bigger picture of my life and beliefs, my internal happiness factor, and my mindset. How tuned in am I to my life, to other people's lives, to what I call God/my Higher Power? How am I tuned into being of service that day, and to be in service that moment? It helps me tune in to look for people, places and things that are messages or lessons for me as a spiritual human being. I explore from deep inside as well as the most expansive view I can muster. I can draw upon these views and messages for confirmation of goodness in people, of clarity in my direction or my path. This helps me see seeds of wisdom that I glean from listening to people and their reactions, or their comments, advice, or how they react or don't react. In those moments, it's a real expression of life at work every day. Being aware of sun, sky, green grass, birds and clean air is part of my day. I live at ground level, but keep a global universal perspective. Luckily I live by the ocean in California where I actually have the power anytime to drive by or be on the ocean or around the ocean, and I understand the magnitude of that thinking. There is something much bigger than ourselves. We are a piece of a much bigger thing, but integral to it all.

I don't think there is anyone I have ever met who can stand on a cliff overlooking an ocean or at the water's edge, or be in the ocean, and not understand and believe how miniscule we are as people and individual human beings, but how necessary we are to the overall big picture. We are big and small at the same time, but when you are at the water's edge of the ocean, you clearly get and understand the ebb and flow of tides, of energy, the give and take, and going forward and backward of life. I love tapping into the environment around me and the bigger global picture, and figuring out how it fits into my life, and how I view the world.

The Collective Sum of All

Many definitions of God as a higher being are held by as many different people as exist. My own personal definition is, "The collective sum of all that is in this and all universes".

When we talk about the power of consciousness, power goals and the power of intention, one can make the point that everyone has free will. We heard this so many times and I believe it to be true. While we're creating our world and trying to find ways to transition, transform, and evolve we have to understand the chemistry and alchemy of all that really is in the big picture. We also have to understand the practicality of our efforts. I believe it's the power of the uniting your clear and specific free will with your understanding and knowing of your higher power, which I will call God, the infinite power. When these two things collide and are mixed together, and we are doing this in intentional ways, it is amazing what you can manifest and create in your life in the world. This is a true secret and the essence, I believe, of what the alchemists were doing.

When you hear about turning 'lead into gold' throughout this book, please remember that it's not always the material and physicality of the minerals, lead and gold, that is implied. It is obviously just a metaphor to be used in describing the power that you have within yourself to create and manifest anything you desire. You are the alchemist of your own life. You are in your own laboratory with all that you need. This has been gifted to you. You have all the necessary elements right before you, and you will find your own special formulas that allow this to work deeply and fully in your own life. Seek and find ways to create your own magic potions and formulas that reflect the unique human and spiritual being that you are.

You can truly create the world you desire and turn any situation, hardship, tragedy, opportunity, or dream into the true gold you desire and deserve. Be clear on it is that you want, and find your true path that serves you with the highest level of what you want. Find the path that creates the most joy in feeling of purpose in your life. This is where you will find your true personal legend. Just as Santiago in the book The Alchemist learned so much from all of his travels and the people he met along the way, so will you. You must travel each and every road yourself with your own compass and with your own instinct. I hope you will rely on the guidance and support that is invisibly around you at all times. When you tap into the offering in this gift you will truly have an easier and more meaningful journey.

Remember it is not the final destination that will give you the greatest reward and the biggest pot of gold. It is all of the wonderful people you will meet that have many gifts and lessons for you if you open your eyes and heart to them. Your interactions with each, your love, your forgiveness, exploring your curiosities and passions, will be the most fulfilling for you each and every day of your life. I hope you will create and pursue big dreams, live your life fully out loud, and be of service and inspiration to others. The world needs what you uniquely can create and offer. I hope you will share with us all of your gifts. And I know in doing so you will have more gold in all the areas of your life that you desire. Enjoy the journey!

Leadership and Spirituality

I have explored my own path of leadership and spirituality in a simple understanding of Shakespeare. He says, "All the world's a stage." As a salesperson, manager, leader and as an executive and entrepreneur, I have used that phrase many times. I believe that we are all acting out parts here on this planet in this particular lifetime, of what it is that we are here to do and what we can learn and give. I realized that whether I was in the hotel/restaurant business, management, in overseeing comedy clubs and as it eventually evolved into real estate, what those pasts were all about on my path. They were an excuse to show up in the world, to make an impact, to grow, to be a better human being and a spiritual being. It was about having interactions with others who were in my view, an expression of higher purpose and higher understanding sometimes beyond my own view. I believe that is the way of energy in our world, whether it is Mother Nature or God or just the energy itself. Energy is constantly changing, evolving and constantly ebbing and flowing.

I believe the exchange with others and how we live our life is an expression of that energy manifesting itself and transforming us. It's not unlike a tree starting to poke up from the ground and sprouting little green stubs, eventually growing into the trunk, branches and soon a recognizable tree. This is still part of growth, an unseen energy fueling and of this particular tree being called forth. One unique seed planted in the soil nurtured by water, sun and time, the tree evolves and grows. It just knows how and when to grow. It doesn't need to try. It is predetermined in its makeup and chemistry to be that tree. I think the interaction that we have in our jobs, careers, companies and our businesses are expressions of this. I have always looked at my path being a leader and in recent years I have started to call myself a servant leader or a Leader of Service. That helps me stay clear finding my path to the right voice and to the right messages that pull me forth into my next steps. The service is to my higher power, God and to the people I can benefit and service.

Eckhart Tolle talks about focusing on the present moment in his book, *The Power of Now,* as popularized by Oprah. The book reminds us to find our truest self, be of service to others and try to diminish the ego, sow love of self and find ways to give to and serve others. Here are a few quotes from the book:

> Being is not only beyond but also deep within every form as its innermost invisible and indestructible essence. This means that it is accessible to you now as your own deepest self, your true nature. But don't seek to grasp it with your mind. Don't try to understand it. You can know it only when the mind is still. When you are present, when your attention is fully and intensely in the Now, Being can be felt, but it can never be understood mentally. To regain awareness of Being and to abide in that state of 'feeling-realization' is enlightenment.
>
> All the misery on the planet arises due to a personalized sense of 'me' or 'us'. That covers up the essence of who you are. When you are unaware of that inner essence, in the end you always create misery. It's as simple as that. When you don't know who you are, you create a mind-made self as a substitute for your beautiful divine being and cling to that fearful and needy self.
>
> Protecting and enhancing that false sense of self then becomes your primary motivating force.
>
> Eckhart Tolle, *The Power of Now*.

I am always striving to focus on living in the present moment, balancing life, spirituality and business, and having a higher purpose message. There is a lot of talk these days about living in the now. This 'living in the now' has gone back to the beginning of time, if you look at any of the scriptures, whether from Eastern or to the Western tradition.

Look deeply at the Jewish, Christian, Hindu or Islam faith, everyone in some fashion talks about being and living in the present moment. Thus man from the beginning of time has tried to like and teach these principles. They word it differently, but sometimes they use those very words. So if you are living in the present moment in your daily life and realizing that there is no past and no future, there is only the present moment, and if you can live from one second, one moment and one hour to the next, that becomes a really interesting way to show up in life. You can simply let life unfold and not only be in the process of what you are trying to create, but also be open to the unfolding of what is in that particular moment.

I have focused my life more and more on living in the present moment, while still planning for the future because those two have to simultaneously exist within both realms. That is just how life functions. I still have desires, goals, wants and needs. But I create them, put them in writing, take action where I can and just let the rest unfold.

Writing in Balance

How do you live within those balances? Part of this for me is by writing down what is important to me. I do annual and monthly fine-tuned goals, business planning, life-planning, affirmations, and various things that help me focus into the clarity of what it is that I am trying to create in my life. This allows me to free up and then go out and create it. I am not in constant strife, worry and question about what it is that I am trying to create. My inner voice, my Higher Power, my trial and error, has led me to creating on paper, in audio files and sometimes on video, what it is that I know I am trying to create and it works very, very powerfully. The power of writing something down, the power of speaking something and then affirming it, and the power of having someone help you be accountable to that, helps manifest everything and makes it be even more rapid in its ability to manifest in your own life. I have heard it said that the power of thought, word, action and deed focused in positive ways help create the life you were destined to live.

My recommendation for someone who wants to create a path in their life, a new business or a new venture, is that you just sit down and start writing it out. You just write and write and write and write with no form or fashion around it. Have an intention in general, knowing that you are trying to create something new, and you are trying to manifest a better situation than you currently have now. Or maybe you are trying to create something that has structure around it that you can then offer to the world to prove it in some way. When you are writing this out and you start running out of steam, maybe speak on some of those thoughts. I love speaking into my phone recorder app and having my spoken thoughts transcribed. It gives a very easy free flow of thought and power.

At this point personally I go back and digest what I wrote. I look for themes. I then try to put things into some type of formation. I break it into chunks which follow obvious areas of my life. For me this is broken down into seven different areas as we discussed in previous chapters: my financial life, spiritual life, family life, health and fitness, community, and my education and higher path. If you are breaking things down into these particular categories, you can then start creating a life plan where you are writing down what you are trying to create. Once you define this, the next thing to do is take each segment and break each one out further. Then you start going back through them and figure out what you really want in more detail.

Brian Tracy, who I shared has been a mentor and friend of mine for many years, has a great thing that he calls diamond mining. This is where you rate yourself on a scale from 1-5 on various categories and it is in the shape of a diamond. Seven are broken into four different points of the diamond, but you rate yourself and then you connect the dots. You are in reality creating a visual as to where your life is in focus. Is your life in focus in terms of family, life, fitness, finances and career? Where is it out of balance? When you look at it, it should be a perfectly shaped diamond that is at the farthest outstretch that it can be, or does it look more like an upside down triangle that has a small point on it that is really out of whack? I have included samples here.

DIAMOND MINING

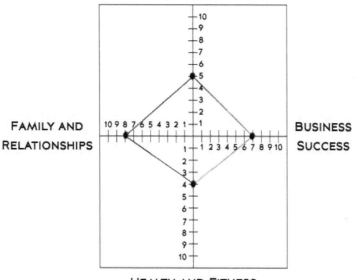

FINANCIAL INDEPENDENCE

FAMILY AND RELATIONSHIPS

BUSINESS SUCCESS

HEALTH AND FITNESS

STRONGEST AREA? 8 - family and relationships

WEAKEST AREA? health + fitness

ACTION COMMITMENT: hire a personal trainer by 2.1.2015
go minimum 3x per week
and cut out late night eating after 8pm

start weekend kayaking with my wife
first time 2.10.2015

Complete Data Mining Example. To receive a blank form that you can print out, please visit leadtogoldbook.com/giveaway

If you are rating yourself in these particular categories, health and fitness, finance, business and spirituality, it is a great place to know where you are starting before you jump into a business life plan. This can help you know where you might need to have a little extra work within your own life before you try something as robust as creating the next chapter of your life or business. When you've got the balance and you've got the plan, you then want to break this into a specific plan. For now, let's have this be the operating system of your daily life. Notice how having a plan leads to being present now.

Decide how you can have written plans, goals and drive for successes, but also allow for living in the present moment.
  Life happens while we make plans, so allow your plans to evolve and mix together in a formula that works in the alchemy of your actual life. Create your own unique '*Lead to gold*'.

EXAMPLE

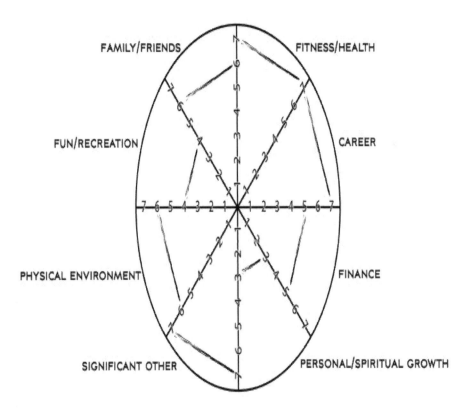

Complete Wheel of Life Example. For a blank version, visit leadtogoldbook.com/giveaway

Inspired Business Planning

When you write your business plan, you obviously have to know what field you are going to be in, whether it is real estate, the restaurant business, the financial industry, or perhaps Internet marketing. I hope that you have done your homework. You obviously have to do market research to check out who the competitors are, what products already exist in the marketplace, and what the existing business models are in that industry. You probably have knowledge of this already if you're already in that field, and you have a sense of history from being in a career on that path. In addition, you can research online through Google, YouTube and Internet searches. Check out businesses, look at their business models, read their mission statements, look at their videos online, and look at their Yelp reviews.

Look at what type of response they are getting, how long they have been in business, and how rapidly they have grown. Do some research so that you know who your competitors are in your immediate market, and also the larger market of that industry. This is a key factor. Research what you are stepping into, what exists and what doesn't. If you believe that your business model is already fine-tuned because you have done the homework, great. Then you know what your product offering is and what your value proposition is going to be to your consumer.

One of the main things I think consumers are looking for is something that makes their life easier, something that is simple to use or that is going to add value to their family or themselves. They want a very fair price that is competitive. If you are in a high-end luxury type market, where people are willing to pay for luxury items, trips, or real estate, then that is a different segment. People are willing to spend discretionary income for high value items as long as they feel they can't get it anywhere else, that it is exclusive and rare. Anything that is luxury or expensive has to be rare. There has to be a premium involved for those who can either afford to get it, or to those that will receive it. There is only a certain amount of this type of commodity that can be bought. This is why the luxury market is a whole other segment. It is a very fun and interesting market, whether you are in real estate, luxury travel or luxury investments.

Once you have done your market survey you need to look at your business offering. How will you distribute your product? How will you get the word out to the consumer? Is that retail? Is it online? Is it a service business? Is it a product business? Understand your distribution vehicle so you know how you are going to get this particular product out. Old traditional marketing is still somewhat viable and can still work. Current marketing practices change every day. Online social media and mobile marketing are taking the world by storm, and these tools are only increasing in availability and usage.

Some questions to consider: What is your combination? How you are going to get your message out to the consumer? What is that message? What are you offering, and how is that different from your competitor? What is your value proposition? What is your elevator speech? Think of your initial conversation about your business to someone new as if you were going in an elevator with someone for 1-2 floors. How can you tell them about your product or service if you had face-to-face time with them for only about 10-30 seconds? If it is online, how can you talk about it in the blink of an eye? What images will you be using from your marketing standpoint? In getting your message out, there is obviously a whole section of business planning that has to go into marketing, advertising and promotion. Understand how to best appeal to your potential consumer through those various vehicles.

Within your business planning process, once you understand your product offering, how it is going to be distributed, and your marketing and your team, then you can start getting into the pricing. What will your product cost? Is it a service product offering, or are you selling a tangible product? What is the cost of your product or service, and how competitive is it compared with other products on the market? Do you know what your cost for your product or your service is? If you were to sell one widget, a pencil, a cup or a pizza, what is the retail cost for that? What is your actual cost? What is your hardcore cost? You also want to know the difference between the margin of your product offering, your return on your investment, and what your gross sale is on it versus your net profit on that particular item.

If it is a service business and you are working on commission, or you are working on consulting fees, what is the income per client/relationship and how you would actually monetize that? What is your margin on that item? Once you have these numbers, your potential gross item number for either gross revenues on the product or the service, then you can break it down and figure out what your net margin is. You can start understanding what the revenue side of the business can be by figuring out how many sales you would have in a day, a week, and a month. You know that is going to ramp up each month, quarter, and each year, and you can start backing anticipated growth into your forecasting. You simply ramp that up to understand what you can maximize.

For example, let's say if you are selling a computer for $500 and it cost you $200 to make, you have 150% profit margin. You are planning to sell 100 computers in the first month, and you plan to increase your sales by 20-30% every month for the first year. You have your gross number and your net number. That is a great way to start, because then you know what your overall revenue will be and you can start figuring out what your cost will be.

There are tons of documents you can get that show what your expenses will be. Your two highest numbers are rent and personnel, especially if you are a brick and mortar business. Next is advertising and marketing. From there it goes down the list with many, many categories that you would create for expenses. You will need to be clear about the monthly and annual expense on what it might cost to run this business. You also need to know what you have to come up for start-up capital. Start-up capital will often be the one-time expenses needed for deposits, equipment acquisition, domain names or other items needed in your particular niche.

Once you plan your revenue and expenses, then you begin to see your potential gross and net profit. From there it is easy to start projecting out what your profits would be in this business in the first year, or two or three. You can have an accountant or a financial person help you with an Excel template to create a projection. There are many business-planning forms online that can help you create these plans. Use these resources to start getting a picture of the business you want to create. You will fine-tune those numbers over time, and this will help you figure out how much capital you need to do this business. You need a clear idea of what you're walking into before your commit real resources to your project. Then think seriously about how and why you chose any particular source of funding. Are you going to be using your own capital that you have from savings, are you going to mortgage your home, borrow from friends and family, take out a loan from the bank, or are you going to get investors?

It is important to dream big dreams, and it is equally important to bring those lofty dreams down into hard numbers, plans and processes. You will be continuously balancing both worlds the entire time you're starting, growing and maintaining your business. Choose a business you love!

Golden Nuggets

 Look honestly at how well you lead yourself in order to become a more effective leader of others.

 Step back from your close perspective, and consider your higher purpose.

 Allow yourself creative inspiration as you write your business plan.

 Create a detailed business life plan aligned with your values and goals.

Chapter **13**

Commitment and the Entrepreneurial Mind

Commitment and Habit

One of my mottos is, "I have to earn my meal". I practice this in several ways. Commitment and habit are key components in my ability to consistently focus on the daily tasks I've chosen to help me stay true to my larger goals and dreams.

Tonight I got home after driving 3 ½ hours to Los Angeles and 3 ½ hours back. Being in a car for 7 hours plus a 3-hour meeting didn't give my body much opportunity to move around. I did my workout this morning, which is great, but I'm committed to exercise in some fashion twice a day.

I usually make sure I'm home comfortably exercising before I cook and eat my dinner. One fairly easy option is to go walk/run to the dog park or to the beach. Sometimes I allow enough time between meetings for this. But today was busy, it is now 10 o'clock at night, and so far I know I'd only exercised once. I grab my tennis shoes, take off my suit and change into casual clothes. I grab the dog because I know Olivia will want to get out to the dog park. Off we go with a flashlight, dog and strong intention to achieve my daily goal and honor my commitment to myself. I'm sitting here now, overlooking an overcast night over the Pacific Ocean, doing my audio notes for some clarity as I'm writing this book. I could have just passed and had a great excuse, but I knew I promised myself and health coach I would exercise twice a day before I ate my last meal of the day and say, "I earned my meal".

Another aspect I committed to in my personal plan is a healthy, clean eating plan, which, right now, is vegan as you know now with no grain and no fruit until I get to my desired base weight. I chose a vegan plan after seeking the advice and direction from a doctor and holistic health expert, Dr. Bernard Meltzer in Del Mar. After becoming a noted surgeon in his early years in San Diego, he made a radical shift. He decided instead of cutting people open and trying to fix people after the fact, that he would change and transition his life and do his best in preventing illness ahead of time.

For forty-plus years he has now helped thousands of people gain extraordinary results in advising plant based diets and using acupuncture to aid in the energy flow of their bodies. I knew this would be radical and intense, but decided to give it my best shot. So I jumped in with both feet cold turkey and became a vegan. Talk about transition and transformation! I had a clear intention of turning my own 'Lead to gold' regarding my health and personal self-care commitment.

I plan to stay on a vegetarian or vegan plan once I hit my goal weight. Right now I'm about 10 lbs. from my goal weight to get down to 175 lbs. When I get to 175 lbs. I'll assess it from there. Every day I'm eating cleanly. I'm eating on point 98% to 99%, and some days to 100% of my plan. So I'm feeling really good about staying committed and creating a new habit in my life.

I have heard it said habits can be formed after 21 days. I think it takes at least 90 days. Some people say it can take up to three years to really form a natural habit that's as implanted as brushing your teeth. I have a long way to go I guess before this is completely in my brain and ingrained in my heart and soul. But right now, it's in my daily practice, which is working great. I am now going on eleven months and have amazed even myself as I've stayed on this intense new plan.

This commitment that I'm making, which is why I'm walking tonight, is clearly forming a habit. Many of us have had vinyl records in the old days when we used to have music albums. The albums would have the little grooves going around the center of the flat disk in a spiral. The music was embedded somehow into the album, into those grooves. Every song, every note, every voice of that song is in that piece of vinyl, seared into the memory of that final album disk.

That's what has to happen with our brains as well. We have to think, speak, and act, and we have to do the deed repeatedly and repeatedly before it becomes ingrained into our consciousness so it is a part of who we are.

You may be focused on forming good habits as I am with my commitment to being more physically fit. I also desire to be a more tuned-in spiritual being, and to honor my body as the temple of my soul. I haven't always treated it that way by any means. I've abused my body many times over the years with food, alcohol, drugs or not exercising it. Now I'm really committed to making sure that my body is a temple of my soul. This is a sign and gesture of honoring God because my priority right now is creating a spiritual path in my life that's unprecedented in terms of what I've done in my past. Although I've always been a spiritual person, I am even more committed on a daily basis to this life. I'm now even acting more spiritually by the simple focus of taking care of my body, mind and soul.

Commitment and habit are essential in our personal and spiritual lives. This also ties right into becoming an entrepreneur or staying on the path once you're an entrepreneur. Commitment and daily habit are key towards your own desired success as you develop and refine your good business habits. Being at your best physically will help you run your business better. I sure know it has worked for me and many others I have followed or coached over the years.

Minding Your Business

I'm also continuously reading and studying to improve my knowledge base. This gives me a greater set of resources to draw upon as I build my business and improve my life. Today as I was reading Robert Kiyosaki's book, *Rich Dad, Poor Dad*, I noticed he kept talking about minding your own business. And the 'business' in that particular book is referring to your assets. When you're minding your own business each day, you're minding any assets you have, whether stocks, real estate or businesses that are throwing off profits so you don't have to work in those businesses day to day. Minding those businesses means keeping track of what's going on there. This is not about what people usually mean when they say, "Mind your own business," which means, "Stay out of mine. Don't bother me. Don't give me your opinion."

In minding your own business, as in the audio book I was listening to on the freeway today, it's about minding your business from a business standpoint. I'm being repetitive here. But in minding your own business of yourself, your soul, your Spirit and of your body, it is clearly the thing I'm doing now as I walk the dog at 10 o'clock at night. I didn't really want to do this tonight. Getting a good jaunt in and getting my heart rate up is minding my own body and soul business. I do this by forming habit and commitment—first, commitment and then habit—in a positive way.

Another book that I just started listening to is by Tony Robbins on wealth, and the seven steps to wealth. He talks about creating a consciousness around that, creating compound interest, great investments and saving so your money works for you. He also talks about creating the discipline of investing in yourself, in your family and in retirement. He reminds us how to become financially independent with this simple formula: earn more, spend less and automate the investing process. Your good financial habits will ensure you won't be trading your time for money but your money machine will work for you whether you're working or not. These ideas also flow very well into commitment and habit.

As I start mastering my body and my food, I continually plan. I have to ensure my success, so each day I set myself up for success regardless of the day's circumstances. My commitment is priority and all else flows from there.

Once we start looking at the desire for change and transition, it is good to remember these very basic ways that create positive change. Doing any of these items or a combination can, and I will help you transform your life in ways you desire.

Four Ways to Change Your Life

1. *Do more of certain things.*

We all know what things are better for us than others such as the right foods, exercise, meditation, saving and investing money intelligently. We also know when we show and give love to our families and others that it fuels good and wonderful things. Thus do more of the things you know work.

2. *Do less of certain things.*

On the flip side, what is not working in your life such as procrastination, criticizing others, over spending, too much food, drink, or television watching. Pick a few and commit to reduce or stop them.

3.*Start doing something new.*

I recently took up Kung Fu. I have wanted to do this for years. It has been a childhood memory and desire I never pursued. So now at age 53 I began. I may be the oldest in the class amongst the 12-16 year olds, but I love it. It has fueled a new energy and spark that spills over to other things in my life. What do you have a secret desire to do? Take an art class, start piano, travel, focus on investing, create a new business? Don't wait. Get started now.

4. *Stop doing something altogether.*

What just no longer serves you, period? Is it drinking, a certain friend, sleeping late, eating late at night, smoking, going to bed too late? Whatever it is that is no longer serving you, find a way to just stop. Choose today. Just stop. As Nike so powerfully says, "Just do it."

These four basic and simple tasks are not easy to do, but they work. If you seek change, transition, transformation and ultimately want to evolve to your highest good, I strongly suggest this powerful formula. This combination and chemistry will truly help be the catalyst to turn any 'Lead into Gold.'

Answers to Prayer

I started having even more thoughts about praying for guidance, and asking how I can serve today, and how I can be a better human spiritual being. I often hear people say, "I've asked God and I don't get any answers," or, "I don't know and I keep praying/meditating and I'm not hearing anything." I'm realizing more and more that God seems to be very subtle. But God is in all things, so he's not really that subtle. If you believe God is energy, as I do and God is in every being, every wind gust, every sunbeam, every tree, every animal, every conversation, if God is energy in all things, then God is constantly talking to us.

My definition of God as I stated is "The sum of all that is in this Universe and all Universes."

So, as we're asking for our prayers to be answered, or for direction in our life and trying to find our purpose, I think we just have to keep putting those questions out there. But then we need to listen differently in the silence, or in the obvious knowingness of the Mother Nature conversations that happen every day.

Watch how Mother Nature develops, grows, dies, prospers and births itself. Watch how people show up in your life. Notice what conversations you have daily. Pay attention to the nudges you have, and start learning the language of Mother Nature. When we speak our native language, we just speak that language. We don't think about how it's spoken; we just automatically know when we're in a conversation how to feel through that conversation.

In conversations with God in prayers, there's a knowingness. If you're listening and watching, seeing and being present in the moment you'll be more aware of how the trees bristle in the wind. The sunrises and sunsets are even more magnificent than you remembered. You may notice the sun bounce just so off your windshield. You'll see a little baby giggle, or watch a dog joyfully play with a ball in the yard. You may see heightened spirit in people's eyes. In those moments there's a knowingness that answers unspoken questions. There is a little tug at your heart or your soul that answers your question, or gives you direction on some prompting to take. You may sense a prompting to call someone, to read a book, listen to a song or to write something down. Those promptings are from listening to God and being open and in flow.

This is often an interesting concept for people to get their heads around. It helps me to continue remembering to ask for guidance and direction. It's being given to us in different data points in all times of the day. It's not unlike how we're bombarded in this day and age with information. If you watch TV, there's CNN scrolling along the bottom, there are pop-up windows that display on your computer, there are text messages that come through every hour. We're getting information bombarded to us all day long in technology. We sometimes don't pay any attention because we are just used to it.

In universal communication, this has been happening to us since the beginning of time. That's what Mother Nature and the universal flow does with us. It's speaking to us constantly. But we don't always choose to listen to that language. We act like it's a foreign language. We don't understand it; we tune it out.

If you're in a bus full of people speaking a foreign language that you don't understand, a lot of times we just tune it out and we read our book. We maybe try and pick up a few words, but we don't pay attention to the rest of it. But if you understand that language, you'll probably get intrigued with the conversations you hear, and you might find yourself eavesdropping. I think in the spiritual practice of life, eavesdropping in your own life and your own direction with God and Mother Nature is really what we all are destined to do. I say not only eavesdrop, but insert yourself and start up a conversation every day of your life. I'm just reminding continually myself to be present and aware.

On TinyBuddha.com, Erin Lanahan talks about five lessons about being present:

1. As I rise up into new levels of consciousness, what is no longer in alignment with it or my highest good must fall away.

2. When I feel the anger of the past or the fear of the unknown, I simply find my feet and begin again.

3. Whatever is showing up in your current experience is meant to be there or it wouldn't be.

4. Surrender to knowing nothing.

5. Let go of what you are still holding on to that needs to be released.

My main message in general for you and to myself is to listen for the conversations with God because the messages, data points and information are coming every moment of every day. And for that, I'm grateful. I'm grateful to the Universe and to God for my life as it's flowing forward. I'm grateful for my body, mind, soul and spirit, and that I'm flowing in a really strong and directed place. I know that God is guiding me to my highest good and to my highest purpose.

I hope you know that is happening for you too, whether you see it or not. But if you see it and can be part of it, you can truly find many ways to turn 'Lead into Gold' for yourself and others.

Turning *Lead to gold* in Unexpected Tragedy

As a family we took an unexpected tragic situation and found ways to turn lead into gold even in that. One day everything was fine and normal in our family, and the next day it wasn't. I found myself the previous day running from meeting to meeting, phone call the phone call, feeling like everything was so important and had to be addressed and that there was nothing that could be missed. The next day my beloved wife Mary Lou was in the hospital in intensive care, and suddenly the world stopped and I realized none of the pressing activities of the day before really had much meaning in any way. All of those phone calls, emails and urgent responses that were needed for others took an immediate backseat to all of the hospital and medical issues at hand. Quickly surgeons, blood doctors, trauma nurses and hospital paperwork went immediately to the frontline in my life. All of all the decisions that were immediately at hand for Mary Lou became the most important focus. That was all that mattered: getting answers, giving answers and finding any way I could be of value to aid in Mary Lou's full and speedy recovery, which at the time we did know could even be possible. But luckily, and with many blessings from the many people supporting and helping us along the way, she made it through and the family made it through.

The power of support, the power of prayer, great doctors and nurses created the miracle we so desperately needed and wanted. During that time in each and every hour in each and every day that I spent in the hospital for weeks on end, I knew there must be a purpose. I knew there must be a reason all of this happening to Mary Lou, our family and friends, and I continually focused on finding the good and the goodness in others that I knew was manifesting because of this tragic situation. I found many. The kind and gracious people who gave of themselves in so many ways helped add to the energy and belief that all would be well. In the weeks and months and year that have passed since that tragic day, we have seen many amazing transitions and transformations that came to pass in our lives. Not only was Mary Lou a miracle herself for surviving this life-threatening fluke, but miracles quickly sprouted all around her and in the people that were involved.

Many new relationships were created, relationships were mended, broken family communications were suddenly opened, and so many wake-up calls shared that help change key things in their lives. There was so much good that came out of this very bad and very hard situation. I've known for most of my life prior to this happening that when you have big tragic situations there's usually many gifts hidden inside. You just have to look for them. In this case they were so obvious it was like a spotlight shining on our lives for the weeks and months following.

I think of the day months afterwards when our daughter Nicole was married in October 2014 just after Mary Lou had been released from the hospital and was into her recovery. She wasn't fully up to speed but she was great enough to be at the wedding looking radiant and beautiful as ever. I remember standing with her at the side overlooking the entire reception with our arms around each other, both beaming from ear to ear with our hearts full and overflowing. We just looked at each other and smiled and knew we were blessed. We also knew months before all of these very same people could very well have attended a memorial service for Mary Lou had she passed. But we knew that was not her day and there are many more plans ahead for her. I'm so grateful and blessed to have her in my life, helping me on my path as I transition and transform.

This episode has given us both even deeper meaning and appreciation for life, love, dreams, God and family. We were given a second chance and we know we have a responsibility to turn this knowledge and the deep feelings into manifestation of ways in which we can help and be of more value to others. I believe this is one of the major life lessons that help me to refocus on my new and inspired path as I continue to evolve to my highest good in my own life, my marriage and my work. As I think back it reminds me once again that everything happens for a reason. Everything has purpose, and everything has a deep meaning to call us forward to our own highest good. I knew when challenged at the deepest core level of potentially losing someone I love more than anyone on the planet, that my faith had to endure. I know my universal beliefs and principles at my core level are the only thing that will carry me through and propel me to a new higher place. I take that on with great responsibility and appreciation as I move forward in my life, creating my true expression of myself and my higher mission.

Christmas in June

This was my Facebook post about our experience that morning, June 7, 2014. I called it "Christmas in June."

> *Have you ever heard this used for events, sales, merchandising or just a phrase in general? Well, for me the phrase and picture below ring true more than ever as I almost lost my wife Mary Lou Pugh Rodgers*

yesterday. Mary Lou had some very unexpected post-surgery complications from a good two weeks after she had a routine procedure. Myself, family and friends spent all day and night in the ICU as she battled with massive blood loss and on many occasions the brink of her loss of life. So today, a bright new day when the nurses and doctors say she is stable and progressing with good prognosis it feels like Christmas to me! The best gift ever the 'gift of Life' and the life the person I love most in the world? I am so very grateful to God, the support, prayers and well wishes from my family, friends and associates whose love and energy helped tremendously through this ordeal. That combo along with the wonderful staff of doctors and nurses at Scripps La Jolla Green saved by beloved wife's life. I am eternally grateful and humbled by these gestures, acts and miracles that aided our lives yesterday when we needed it most! So on this Saturday I hope you will help me celebrate life, love, friends and the value and the necessary element in life of Faith! My faith in a higher power and higher purpose sustains and inspires me most days. But I can tell you that the last two days my faith and the gift of life is more clear and valuable than ever before! I hope you will go hug someone you love today, forgive or allow someone to forgive you, accept at a deeper level, radiate your light brightly for all to see and remember we all have a purpose in this life and I hope we

all allow it to achieve its full expression
before we depart this planet, as we all
eventually will do. I just knew and had faith
that yesterday was NOT the day Mary Lou
would be making her exit. So today I will go
hold her hand, kiss her forehead, tell her I
love her and continue to will, pray and guide
her back to full health! We both would
appreciate your continued prayers and
support and will send you ours. Tis the
season and Merry, Merry Christmas to you
all but especially to my love and soul mate
Mary Lou! You are my greatest and sweetest
gift I have ever been blessed to receive!

I'm especially so grateful on this anniversary Christmas in
June week that we have Mary Lou, that she lived, that she's
touched so many people, and that so many have helped us
and our family with prayers and guidance and direction as
we evolved as spiritual human beings over this last year.

As this book comes to a close and we finish our journey
together, I wanted to bring us back around to the start of the
book where I speak of the book "The Alchemist:"

> *In this story, Santiago sets out on his quest for his*
> *own treasure and soon realizes that he is ultimately*
> *finding his own "Personal Legend." In ending this*
> *story, I will briefly summarize a few of the key*
> *points, transitions and transformations that*
> *encompassed the rest of this soulful and universal*
> *story.*

At the beginning of this book we left off this story with the Englishman, a stone, the emerald tablet and Santiago setting out on the journey across the desert. As it turns out, the caravan must make an extended stop in Al-Fayoum in order to avoid increasingly violent tribal wars taking place in the desert. There, Santiago falls in love with Fatima, who lives at the oasis. During a walk in the desert, Santiago witnesses an omen that portends an attack on the historically neutral oasis. He warns the tribal chieftains of the attack, and as a result, Al-Fayoum successfully defends itself against the assault. The alchemist gets word of Santiago's vision and invites Santiago on a trip into the desert, during which he teaches Santiago about the importance of listening to his heart and pursuing his Personal Legend. He convinces Santiago to leave Fatima and the caravan for the time to finish his journey to the pyramids, and he offers to accompany Santiago on the next leg of his trip.

While the alchemist and Santiago continue through the desert, the alchemist shares much of his wisdom about the Soul of the World. They are mere days away from the pyramids when a tribe of Arab soldiers captures them. In exchange for his life and the life of Santiago, the alchemist hands over to the tribe all of Santiago's money and tells the soldiers that Santiago is a powerful alchemist who will turn into wind within three days. Santiago feels alarmed because he has no idea how to turn into the wind, and over the next three days he contemplates the desert. On the third day, he communicates with the wind and the sun and coaxes them to help him create a tremendous sandstorm. He prays to the Hand That

293

Wrote All, and at the height of the storm he disappears. He reappears on the other side of the camp, and the tribesmen, awed by the power of the storm and by Santiago's ability, let him and the alchemist go free.

The alchemist continues to travel with Santiago as far as a Coptic monastery several hours from the pyramids. There, he demonstrates to Santiago his ability to turn lead into gold using the Philosopher's Stone. He gives Santiago gold and sends him off. Santiago begins digging for the treasure at the foot of the pyramids, but two men accost him and beat him. When Santiago speaks to them about his dream vision, they decide he must have no money and let him live. Before leaving, one of the men tries to illustrate the worthlessness of dreams by telling Santiago about his own dream. It concerns a treasure buried in an abandoned church in Spain where a sycamore tree grows. The church is the same one in which Santiago had his original dream, and he finally understands where his treasure is. He returns to Spain to find a chest of jewels and gold buried under the tree, and plans to return with it to Al-Fayoum, where he will reunite with Fatima, who awaits him.

SparkNotes Editors. "SparkNote on The Alchemist." SparkNotes.com. SparkNotes LLC. 2010. Web. 5 Mar. 2016.

This story the "Alchemist" and mine both speak to the power of finding and following your own path, learning, growing and living to the fullest expression as to who you are! They also speak to the power of love and sharing it with your own "true love" and hopefully many others where you can through your life. The journey of life is not always an easy one but it is a fulfilling one when you live fully awake and in search of your highest good and destiny. There will be many teachers, guides and gifts along the way when you open yourself up to them.

I hope you have enjoyed this book and it has stirred something in you to seek out on your own new journey and mission. You know you have something calling you faintly or maybe loudly in the distance. I am sure you know the nudging you have at your back and the pull and tug you have inside your very soul is calling for a reason. A reason and destiny only you can uniquely fulfill. If you are already well on your way on your path and adventure I applaud you to keep going and enjoy every step, every obstacle, every magical encounter. You surely will not have all the answers, you will have road blocks and you will be faced with many fears. Once we have truly, fully and with commitment made up our minds and hearts, the Universe will conspire towards our success.

Here is to you manifesting all the great and full success you deserve while "turning your own lead into gold!"

So today is a great day. Today is a really great day! I have a choice I can be happy or I can be really happy. Today I choose to be really, really happy!

GOLDEN NUGGETS

 Commitment and good habits are key to success as an entrepreneur and in life.

 Following through on our plans even when it's not easy or comfortable is how we stay ahead of the competition.

 Great success comes through our choices all day, large and small, significant or seemingly insignificant.

 Advance your own personal legend in all you do whenever you can.

 Stay open, expect miracles and love!

Ambassadors

This page is dedicated to all the many people that helped me on my path in getting this book created and then fully manifested. There've been countless people along the way helping contribute to this becoming a reality. I recognized some of these individuals at the beginning of the book on the acknowledgment page. They may be mentioned here again but there are others that unfortunately just did not fit in that section. I'm grateful to all of you for your friendship, generosity and your support with your actions, generous time and gifts. I have learned from each of you. I have valued your materials, content and so appreciate you educating me and sharing it with me in my growth and evolution. Also any readers of this book I know you will find value in researching or connecting with any of these brilliant individuals and companies. Check out their sites, mission, offerings and messages.

- Brian S. Tracy
  World renowned speaker and over 70 bestselling books written consulted for more than 1,000 companies and addressed more than 5,000,000 people in 5,000 talks and seminars throughout the world
- John Assaraf, Chairman & CEO, NeuroGym, added to the book the Secret, Wrote the book the Answer, Having it all and various bestselling books. http://www.myneurogym.com/brain-a-thon

- Greg S. Reid, author Think and Grow Rich series. Secret Knock Workshops, Serial entrepreneur, speaker
www.secretknock.co

- Mark Thompson
NY Times bestselling Author, Serial Midas touch investor
Former Chief of Staff Charles Schwab
Worked side by side Steve Jobs, Charles Schwab, and Richard Branson
http://markcthompson.com

- Amateo Ra - Vision Architect- Blogger- Coach. Online courses and brands that thrive
http://amateora.com/

- Mrs. Allyn Reid, Publisher, Producer and Mrs. San Diego 2015. Cofounder of Secret Knock workshops
https://about.me/allynreid

- Fabrice BEILLARD, Globally acclaimed Business Optimization Expert, Best Selling Author, International Speaker
australiabusinesscoaching.com.au

- Barnet G. Meltzer, M.D., F.A.A.F.P.
Pioneer and expert physician in holistic and preventative medicine. Author, talk show host, speaker. http://www.maketimeforwellness.com

- Bill Walsh CEO & Founder Power Team USA
  Voted top 10 business coaches in the US by Global Gurus
  Powerteam International
  http://www.ipowerteam.com

- Dr. Gary Ranker
  Global CEO Coach, speaker
  http://www.garyranker.com

- Dr. Scott & Shannon Peck, Authors, "The Love You Deserve" & "Liberating Your Magnificence"
  https://www.linkedin.com/in/shannonpecksoulmatejourney
  http://www.scottandshannonpeck.com/bio
  http://www.scottandbob.com

- Steven E. Schmitt, Founder of Law of positivity
  Author, Entrepreneur, media expert
  http://lawofpositivity.com

- Marshall Goldsmith
  Voted Top 5 Executive Business Coach Global Gurus
  Thinkers 50 list
  NY Times Best Selling Author Triggers, MOJO, What got you here, won't get you there
  http://www.marshallgoldsmithgroup.com

- Marie Jo Atkins San Diego top Real Estate agent Over 1 billion dollars in real estate sold.
  Pacific Sotheby's Poway California
  http://mariejoatkins.com

- David M. Corbin coach, keynote speaker, author ILLUMINATE, Preventing Brand Slaughter, ReSanity
  http://davidcorbin.com

- Eileen Schwartz, Founder and CEO The Success Table Coaching platform,
  Certified John Maxwell coach
  http://www.thesuccesstable.com

- David Tal and Avi Tal Agentology partners and owners. Reshaping the industry for real estate for Agents, buyers and sellers. www.agentology.com

- Sarah Pugh - M.F.A. Writer, editor, social media marketer. Twitter @sarahtv3, www.sarahtv3.com

- Daniel j. Daou
  DAOU vineyards & Winery
  Winemaker and co-proprietor, serial entrepreneur
  http://www.daouvineyards.com

- Rich German, author of Monetize Your Passion, Cofounder the JV Experience. Top coach, Sea Life lover and advocate
  http://richgerman.com

- Michael Linnard, MCSD
  Little Red Tree Publishing, LLC, editing
  www.littleredtree.com

- Carola Eastwood and Chetan Parkyn
  Coaches, Spiritual leaders, speakers, Human design experts and advisors
  https://www.humandesignforusall.com

- Raul Villacis
  CEO Founder The Next Level Experience, Serial Entrepreneur, Speaker, Coach
  www.TheNextLevelExperience.com

- Marilyn McLeod - coach, writer, author, co-author, social media expert, educator.
  http://coachmarilyn.com

- Leif Andreas Chief Graphic designer and media advisor. Continuum Designcontinuumdesignandmarketing.com

- Jim Cronin Owner/Generally Awesome Great Guy Real Estate Tomato Custom responsive websites and World Class training RealEstateTomato.com

- Lane Ethridge founder of Changing Lanes International, a two-time National Bestselling author, speaker and trainer, radio personality and successful entrepreneur http://www.laneethridge.com http://www.Laneethridge.com/authority

- Haris Reis Vice President of Changing Lanes International, National Best Selling Author, Digital Marketing Specialist http://www.harisreis.com http://www.changinglanesnow.com

- Mo Ranji Founder and CEO Roya Digital Media, Awesome Websites and Social Media https://www.roya.com

- Bernardo De La Vega and Rebekah Rathiga Co-Owners of Multimillion dollar Amazon Business, serial Entrepreneurs. Rebekah is an Instagram celebrity with over 75,000 followers https://www.facebook.com/bernardodelavegacgmI/about https://www.facebook.com/rebekah.letchumanan/about Follow me on Instagram: @RebekahLetch

- Kim Ades, M.B.A.
  PRESIDENT and founder, FRAME OF MIND
  COACHING & JOURNALENGINE™
  SOFTWARE
  http://www.frameofmindcoaching.com/our-team/

- Jessica Rhodes and team Interview Connections.
  Podcast experts and top podcast booking service
  http://www.interviewconnections.com

- Giant Partners media Phil Katz, Sean Chaudhary and
  team. Multimedia and Digital marketing specialist.
  Data and email and mail marketing experts.
  http://www.giantpartners.com

- Ryan McFarland and Kenneth Brown. Real Estate
  investors, Experts, Workshop and education
  providers, online marketing strategist. Commercial
  and Residential Real Estate
  http://www.yourwealtheducation.com

Thanks again to all of you amazing and generous people! I
eternally grateful to each and every one of you!

About the Author

Stephen D. Rodgers and Alchemy Advisors are committed to adding the most value as possible to you. Here is some more info you may find helpful as to what we do.

We are a consulting, coaching & education firm.
We help people & businesses Transition-Transform-Evolve to their highest good in business & Life!

We can guide small and large businesses and help turn lead into gold, challenges into opportunities and dreams into Reality. We use the Alchemy and the right chemistry to create a unique formula just for you and your success!

We have helped startups, midsize and large fortune 500 companies achieve and exceed their goals by using our unique and results oriented systems and formulas!

If you would like some information on life or business coaching, please reach out. There is also a wealth of support on various consulting options and if you want to be part of our upcoming free webinars please register at the website.

There is also a 7-week course starting for a select few very soon. Check it out and if we are a fit we will reserve you a VIP seat in the online course.

Once you visit the site, you will notice a plethora of videos, podcast, free forms and business plans.

We would love to connect on the social media site of your choice. Let's stay connected and let us be part of turning some of your own "lead into gold!"

- www.thealchemyadvisors.com
- Tel: 858.829.2969
- Steve@steverodgerstoday.com
- Skype: srodgerstoday
- facebook: www.facebook.com/steverodgerstoday
- facebook: www.facebook.com/thealchemyadvisors
- Twitter: @srodgerstoday
- www.linkedin.com/in/steverodgers

A little more about Stephen D. Rodgers

Business, lifestyle consultant, and author, Stephen Rodgers is a leader helping others discover, maximize, and increase their highest good and purpose in life and business. Stephen's extraordinarily successful career spans from being a branch manager to evolving to the CEO of a real estate firm generating over $25 billion in annual sales, almost 40,000 transactions, managing a team of 4,600 agents, starting and running his own ultra-successful real estate company and collaborating with the elite. One of Stephen's career highlights was meeting and working for Warren Buffett for many years.

His inner circle includes many great leaders such as John Assaraf, Brian Tracy, Marshall Goldsmith and Mark

Thompson. His wife's life threatening health crisis was the impetus for Steve to switch to giving back and helping others achieve their dreams. Steve is happily married with adult children and grandchildren. He has committed to a vegan lifestyle for over a year and enjoys traveling, boating, yoga, meditation practices, the arts, films, biking, sky diving, white water rafting and perhaps most of all, kung-fu, his newest passion.

Stephen is excited to be on his new path of consulting, coaching and conducting powerful workshops. He is delighted to join the ranks as a published writer and he looks forward to authoring more books. His mission is to continue inspiring as many as possible to transition, transform and evolve all areas of their lives through turning lead into gold.

Made in the USA
Middletown, DE
06 May 2019